Non-verbal Reasoning

10 Minute Tests

11+–12+ years

TEST 1: Similarities and Grids

Test time: 0 5 10 minutes

Which pattern on the right belongs in the group on the left?

Example

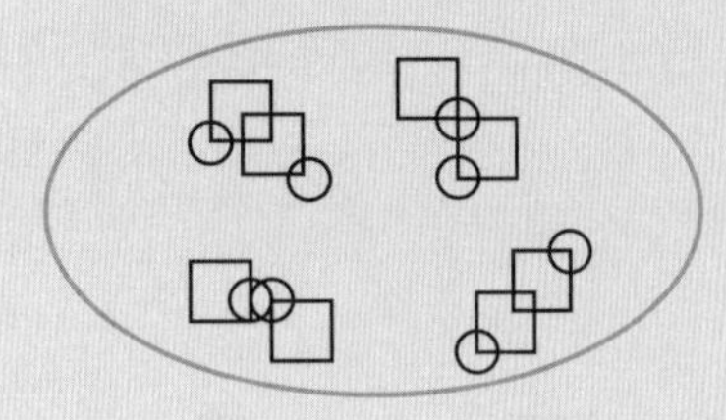

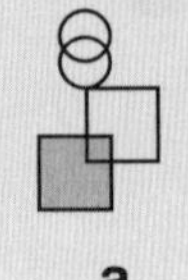
a

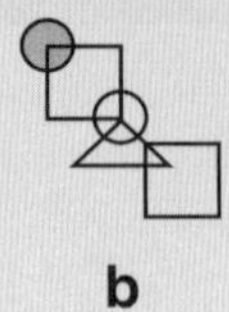
b

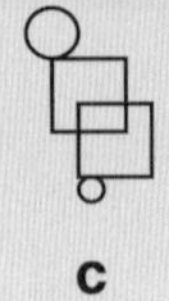
c

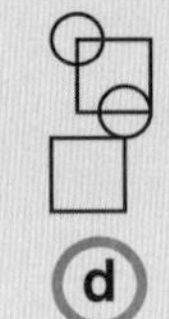
d

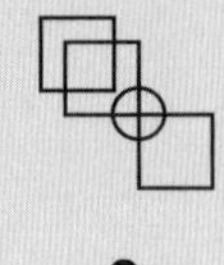
e

1

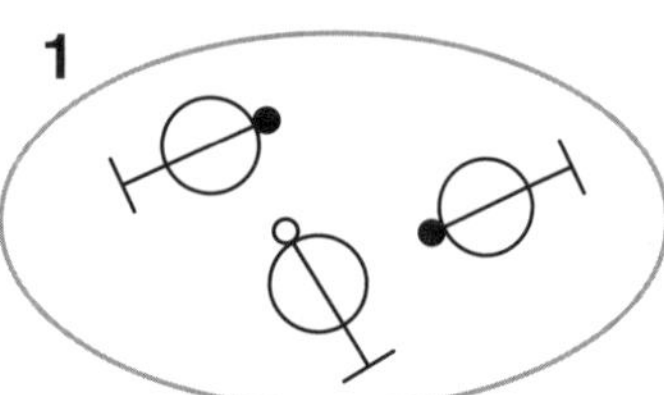

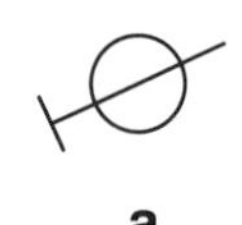
a

b

c

d

e

2

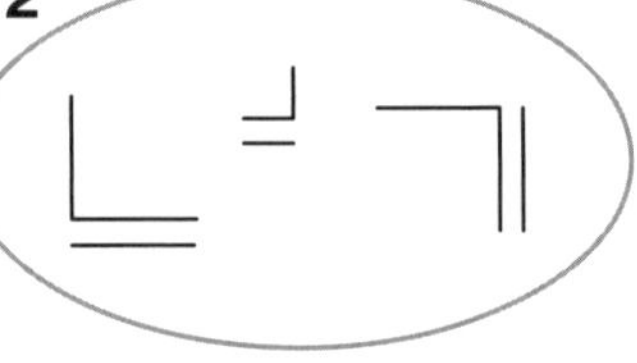

a

b

c

d

e

3

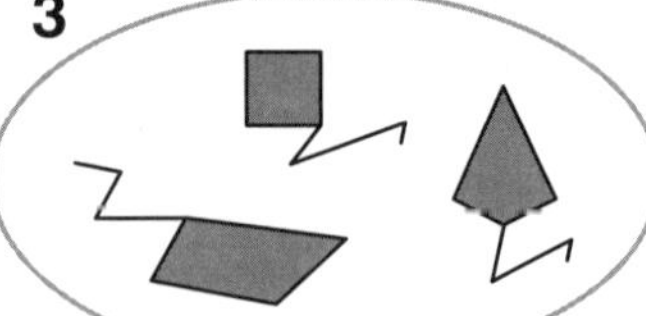

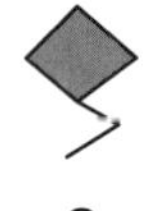
a

b

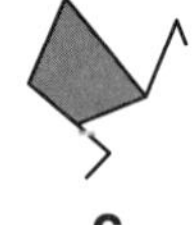
c

d

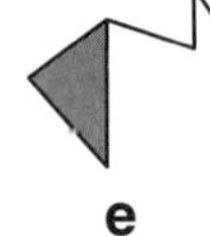
e

4

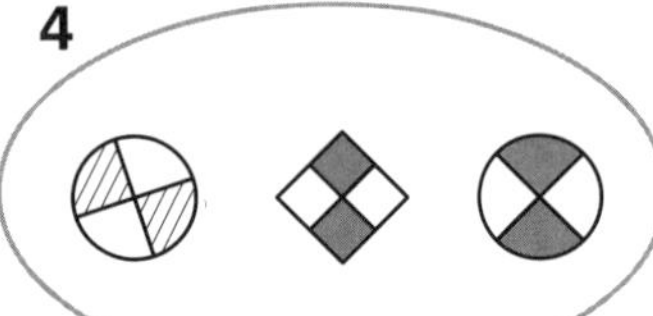

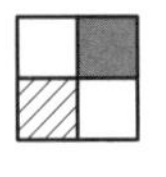
a

b

c

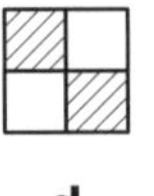
d

e

5

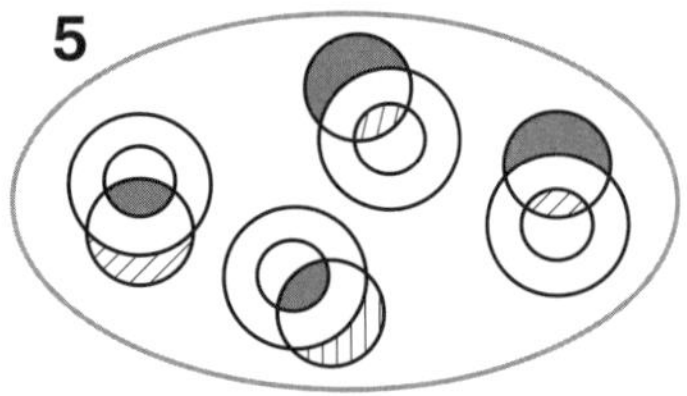

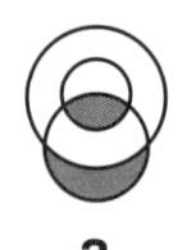
a

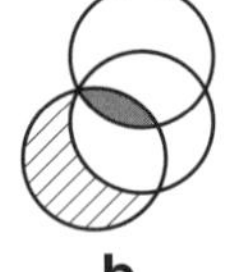
b

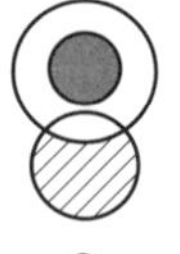
c

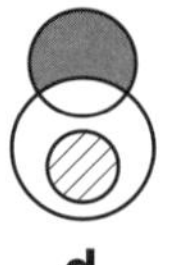
d

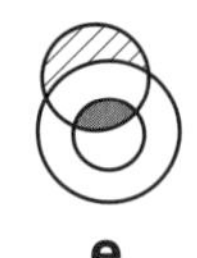
e

6

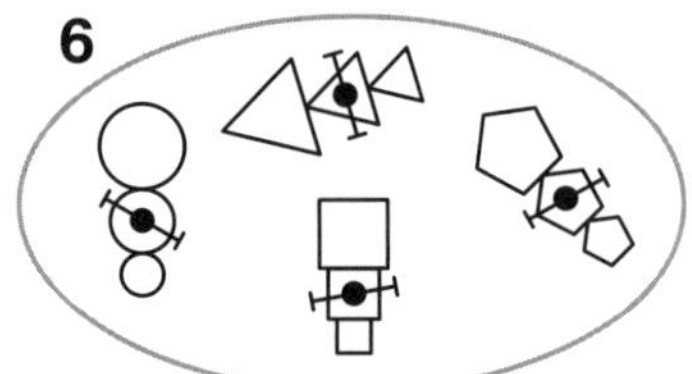

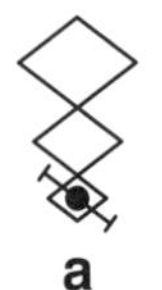
a

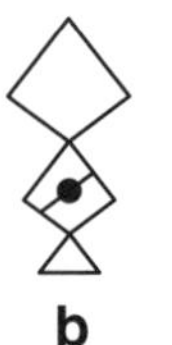
b

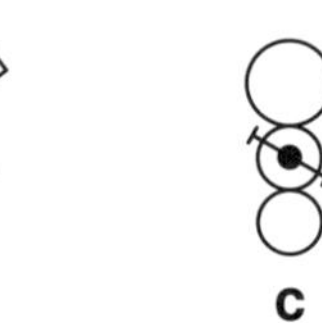
c

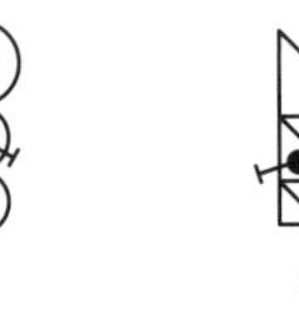

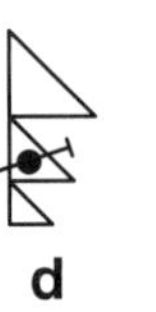
d

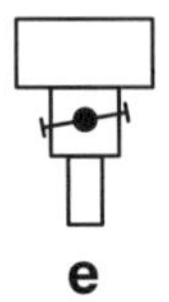
e

Which shape or pattern completes the larger square?

Example

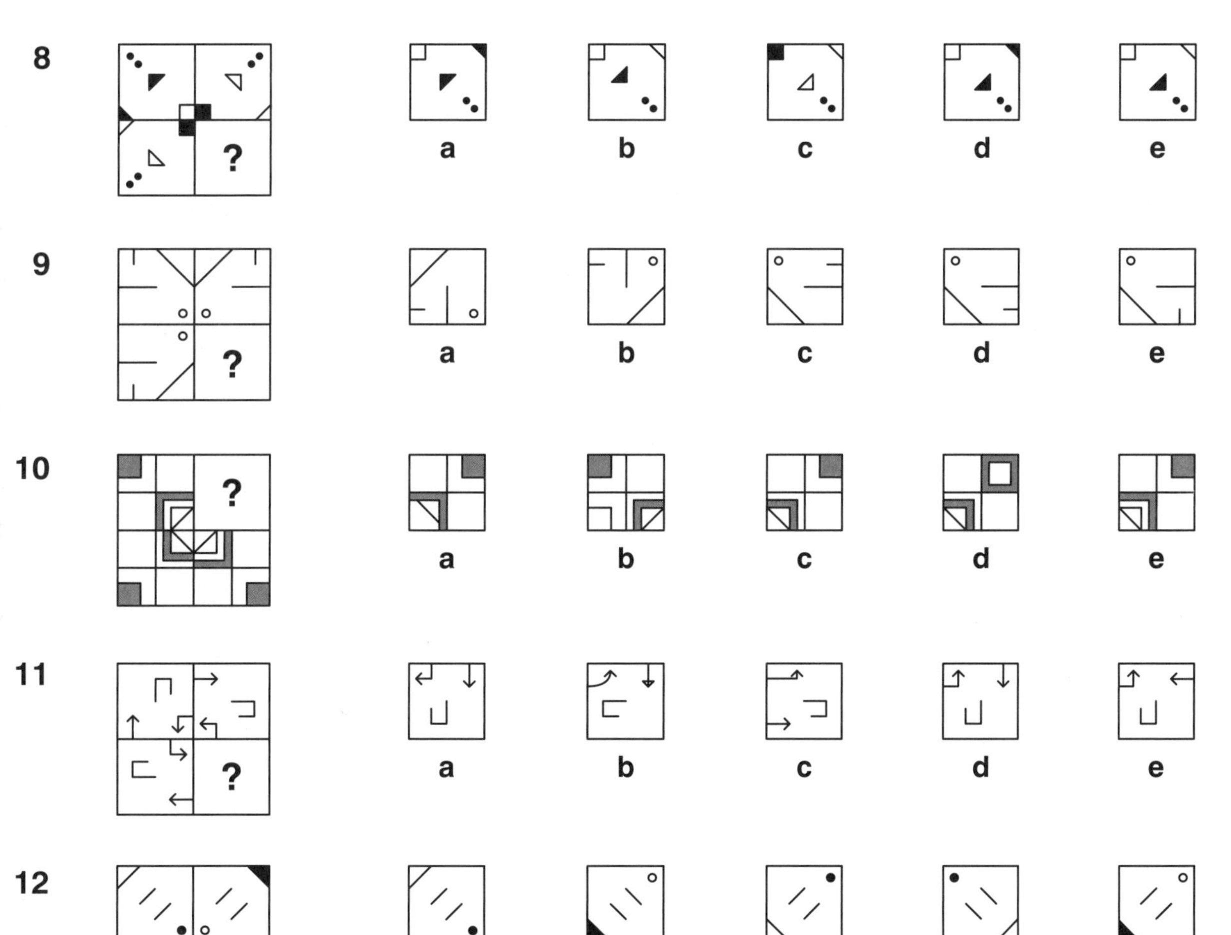

Total

TEST 2: **Analogies and Reflection**

Test time: 0 5 10 minutes

Which shape or pattern on the right completes the second pair in the same way as the first pair?

Example

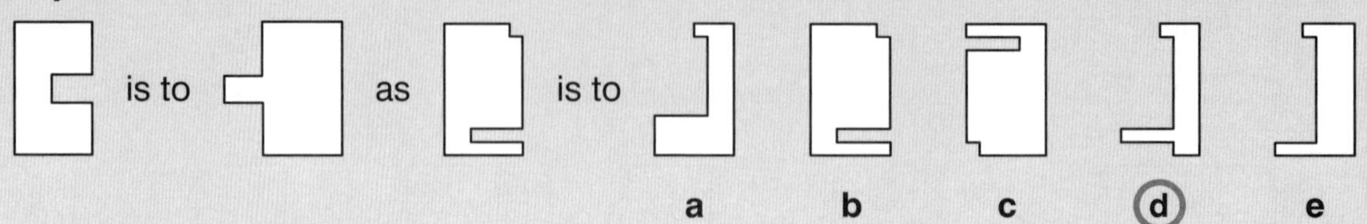

1
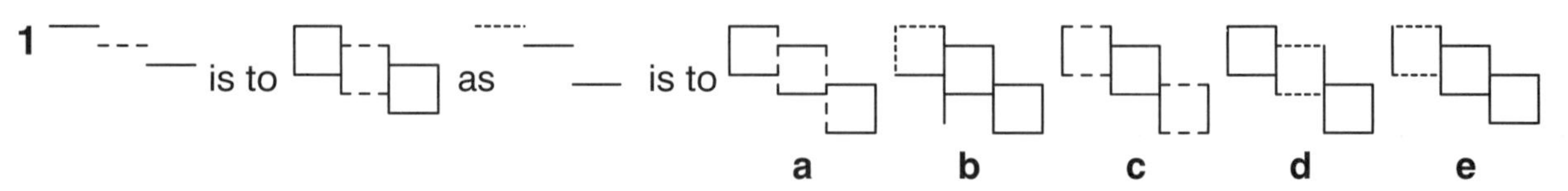

2
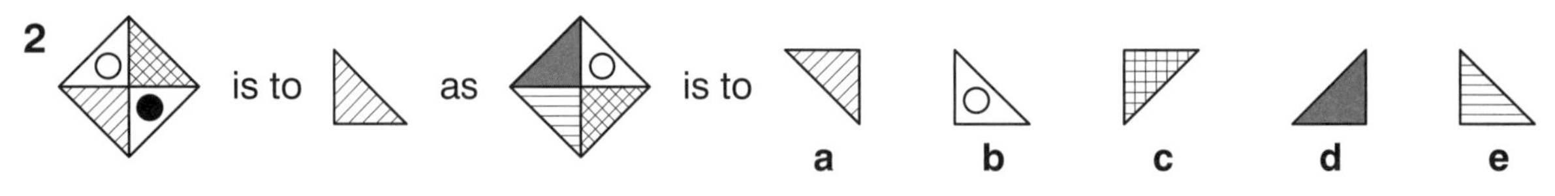

3
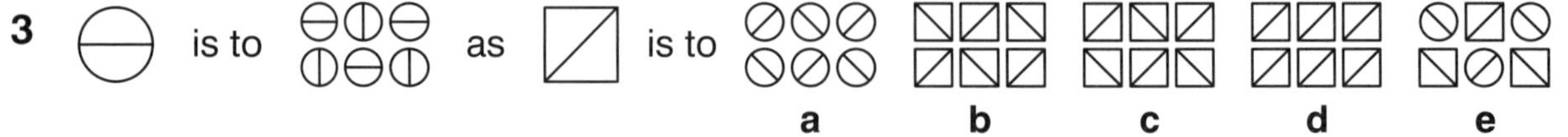

4
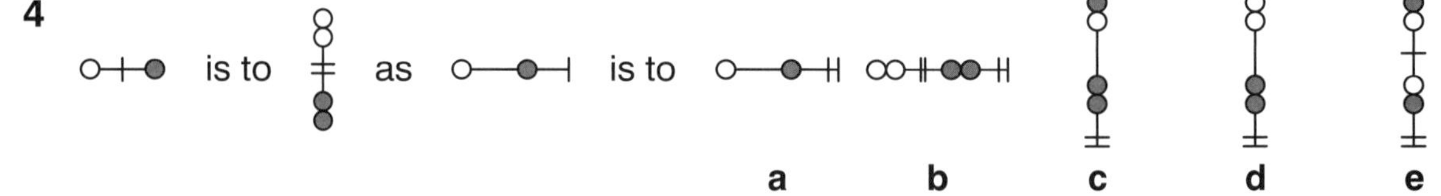

5
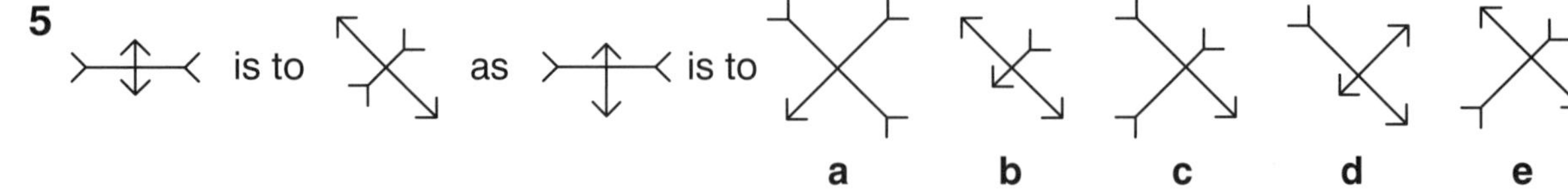

6
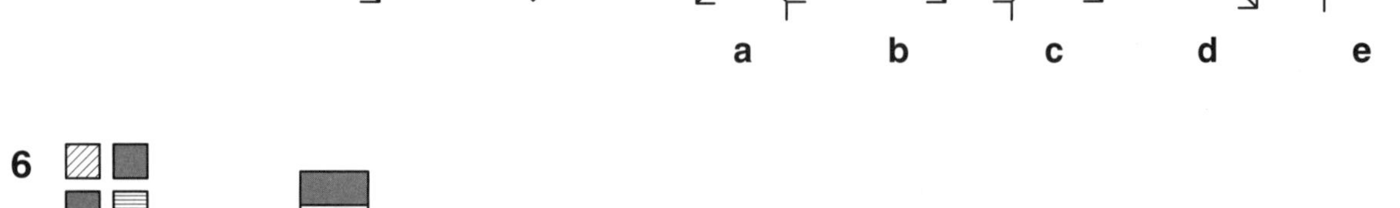

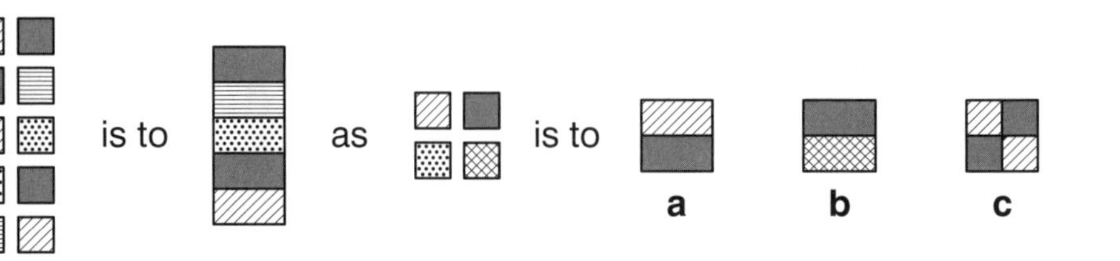

Which shape on the right is the reflection of the shape given on the left?

Example

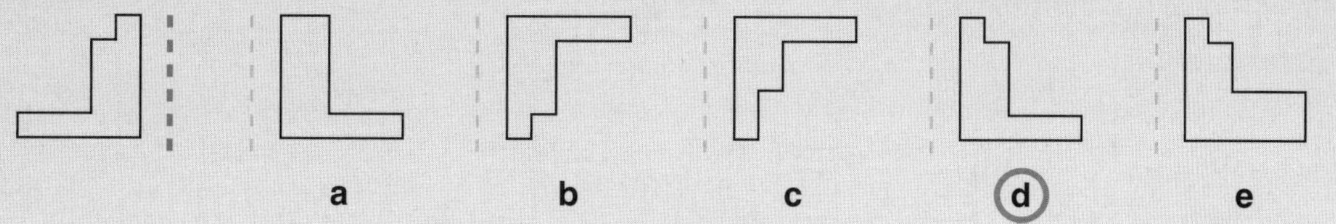

a b c (d) e

7

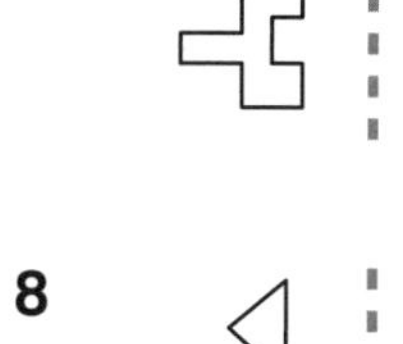
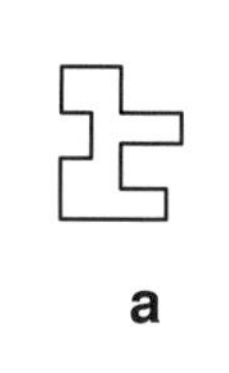
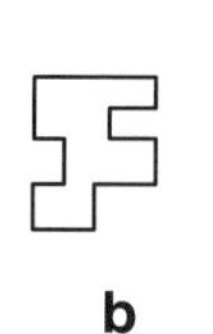

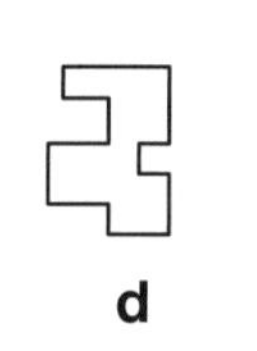
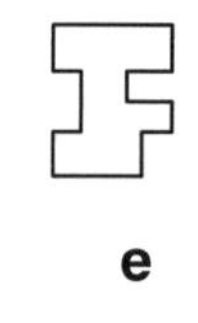

a b c d e

8

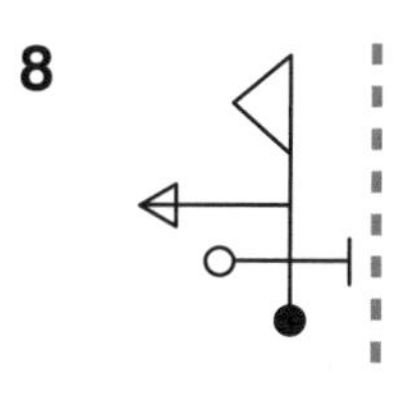
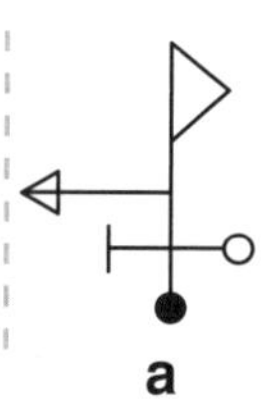
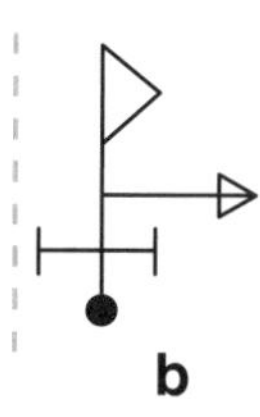
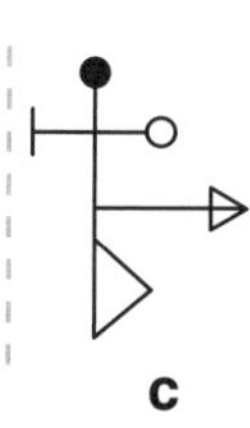
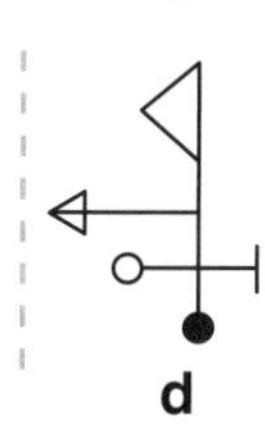
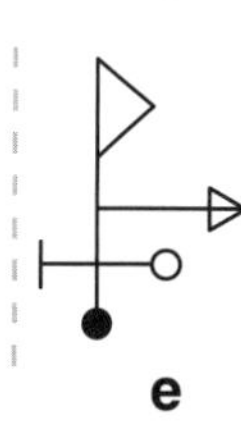

a b c d e

9

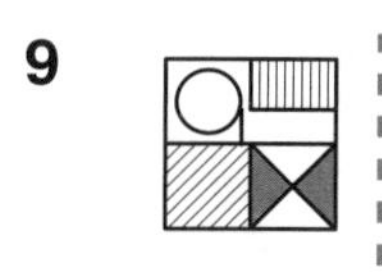
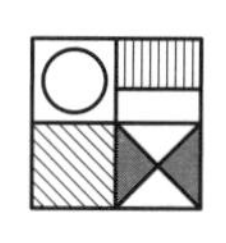
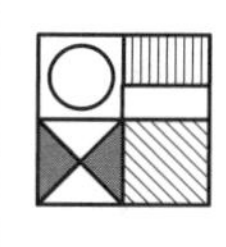
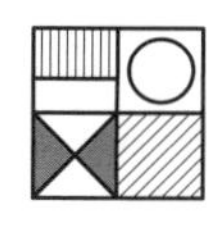
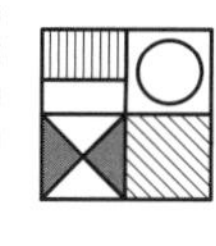
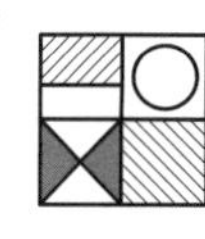

a b c d e

10

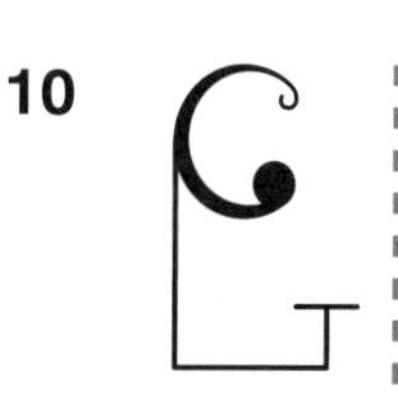

a b c d e

11

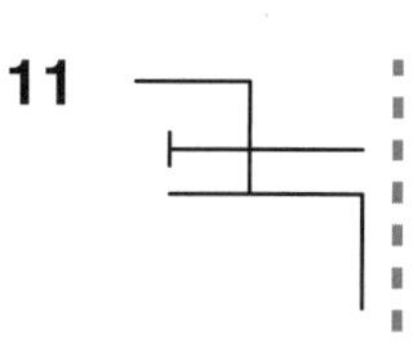
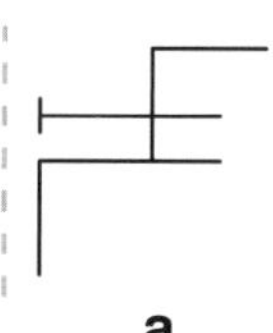
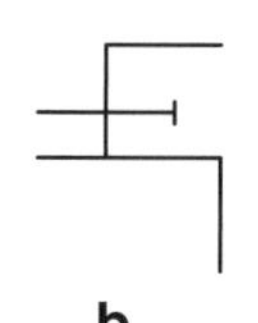
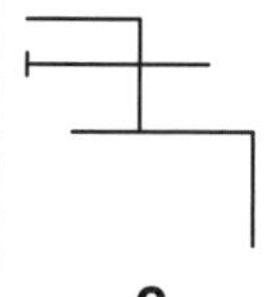
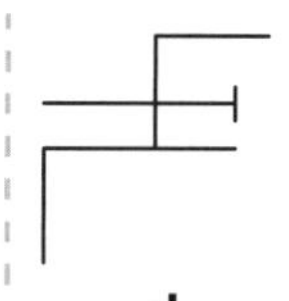
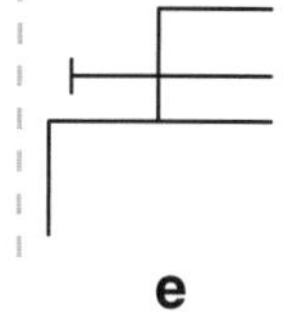

a b c d e

12

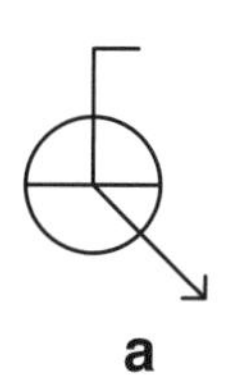
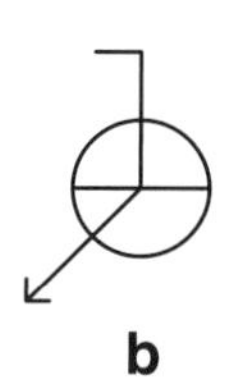
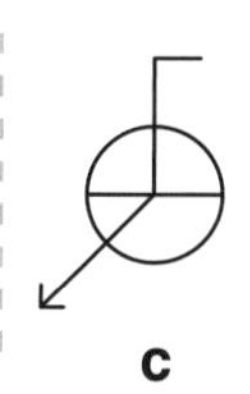
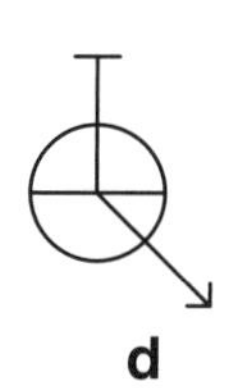

a b c d e

Total

TEST 3: **Sequences and Grids**

Which one comes next?

Example

 ?

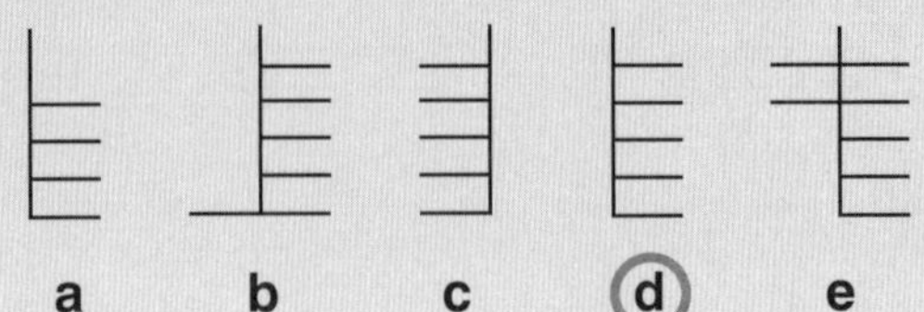

a b c (d) e

1 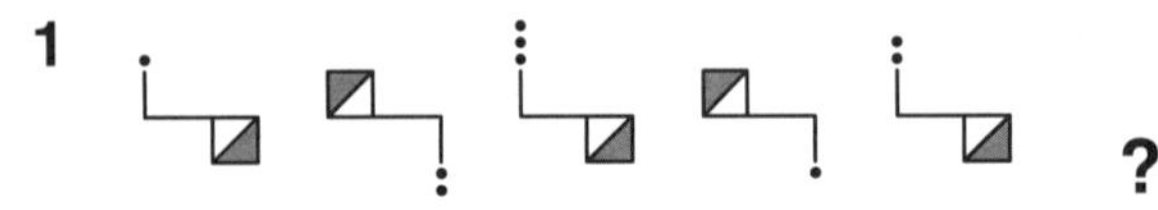 ?

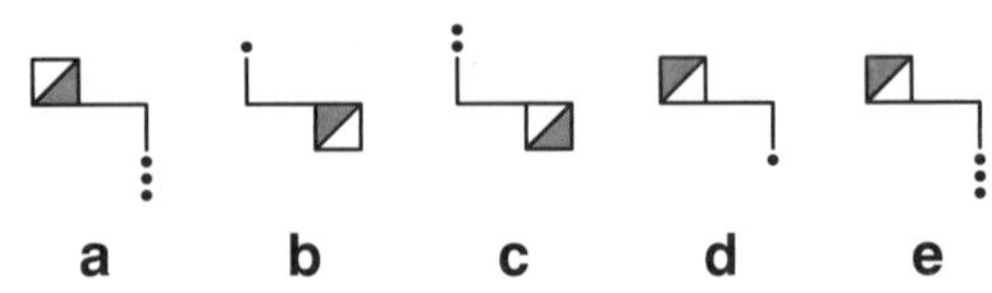

a b c d e

2 ?

a b c d e

3 ?

a b c d e

4 ?

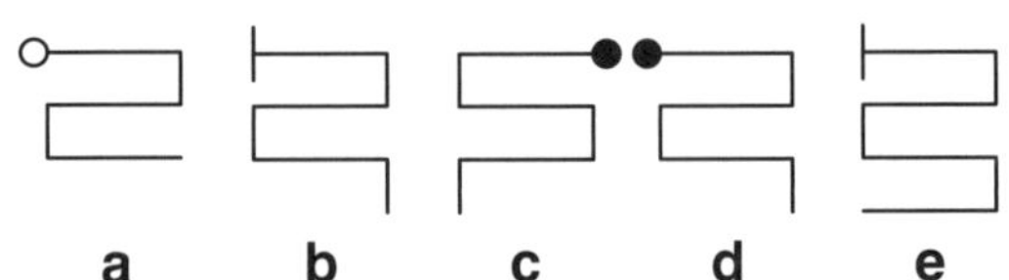

a b c d e

5 ?

a b c d e

6 ?

a b c d e

Which shape or pattern completes the larger square?

Example

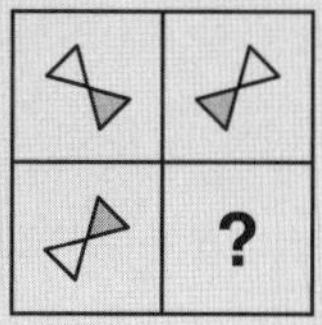

a b c (d) e

7

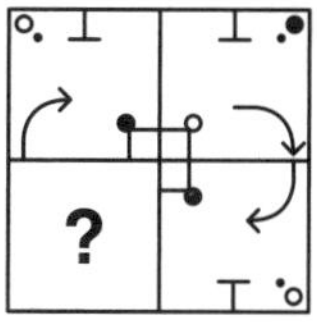

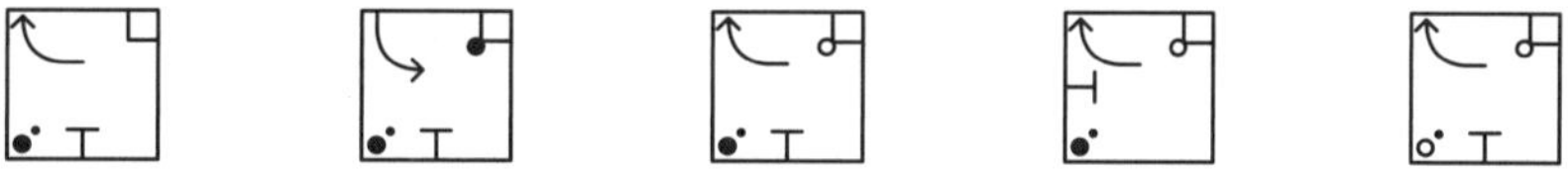

a b c d e

8

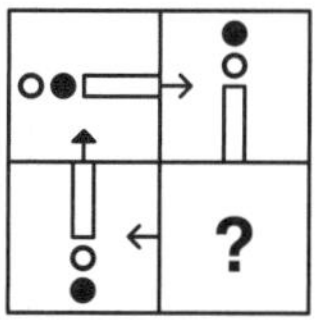

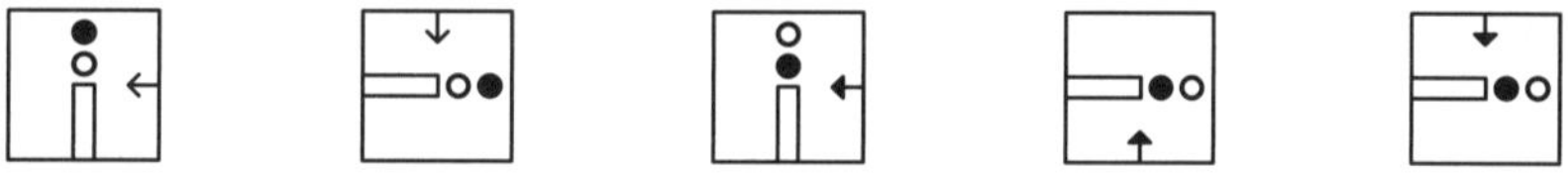

a b c d e

9

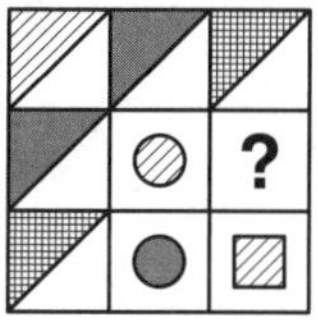

a b c d e

10

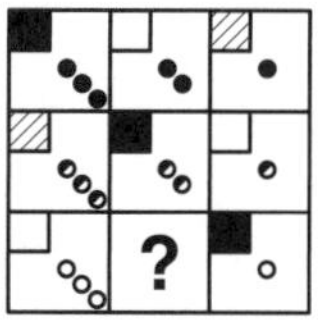

a b c d e

11

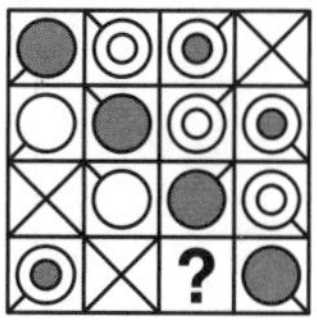

a b c d e

12

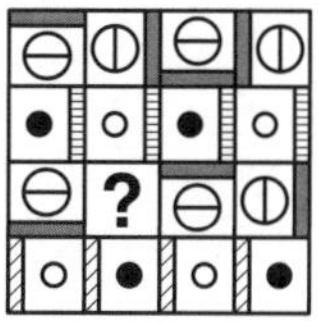

a b c d e

Total

Test time: 0 5 10 minutes

Which pattern on the right belongs in the group on the left?

Example

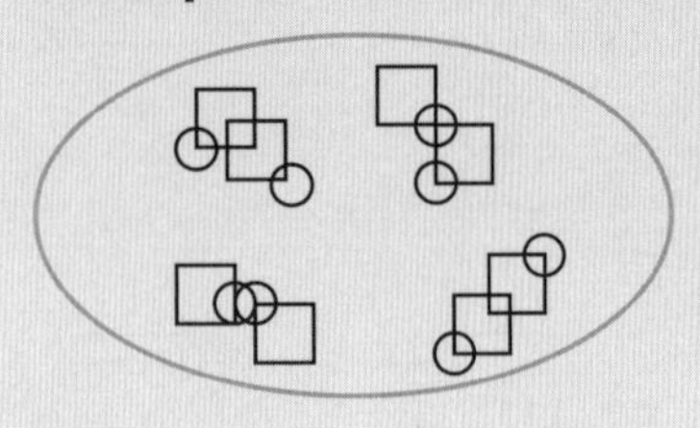

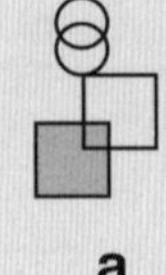
a

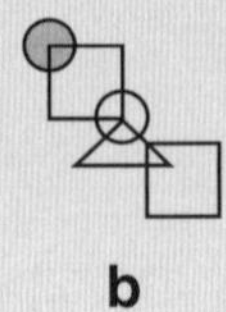
b

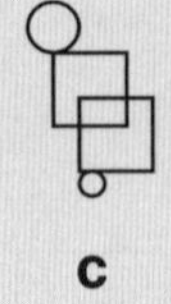
c

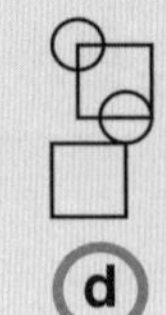
d

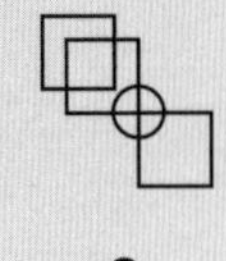
e

1

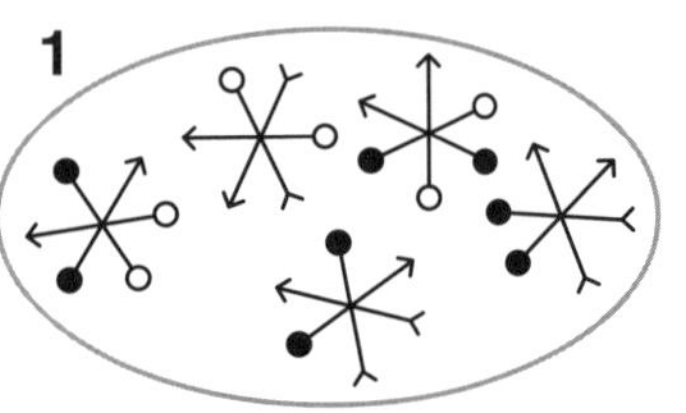

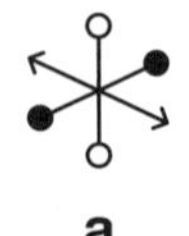
a

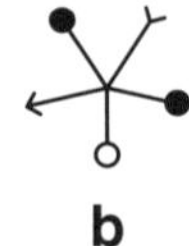
b

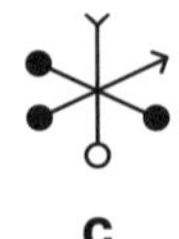
c

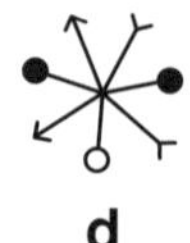
d

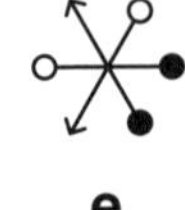
e

2

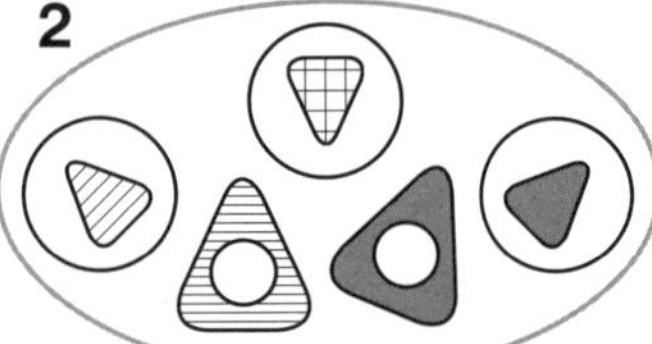

a

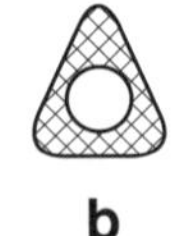
b

c

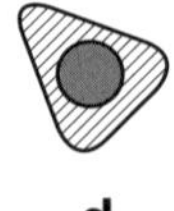
d

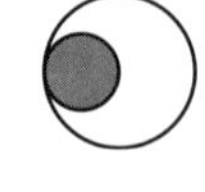
e

3

a

b

c

d

e

4

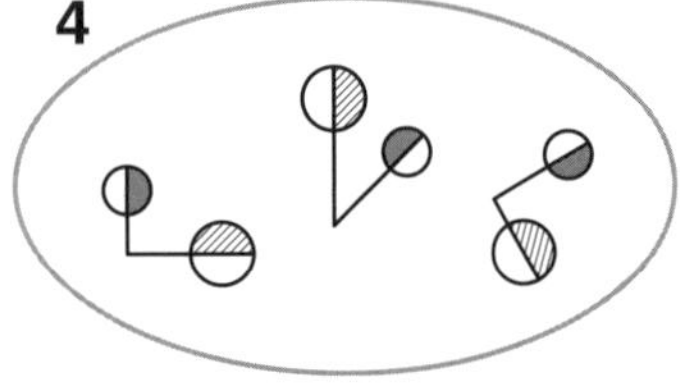

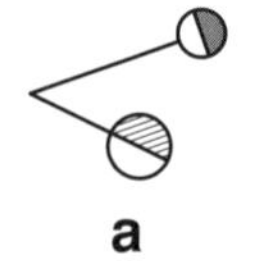
a

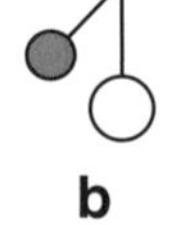
b

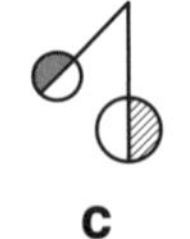
c

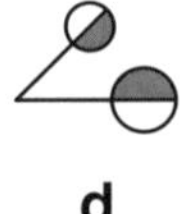
d

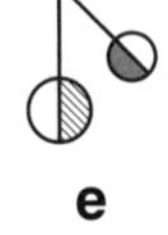
e

5

a

b

c

d

e

6

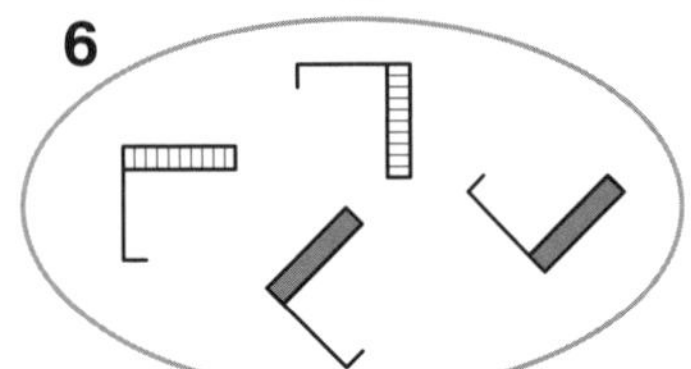

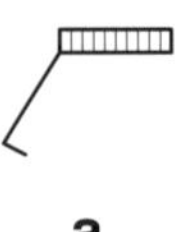
a

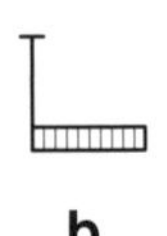
b

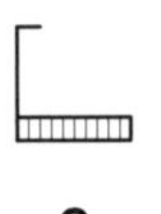

c

d

e

Which code matches the shape or pattern given at the end of each line?

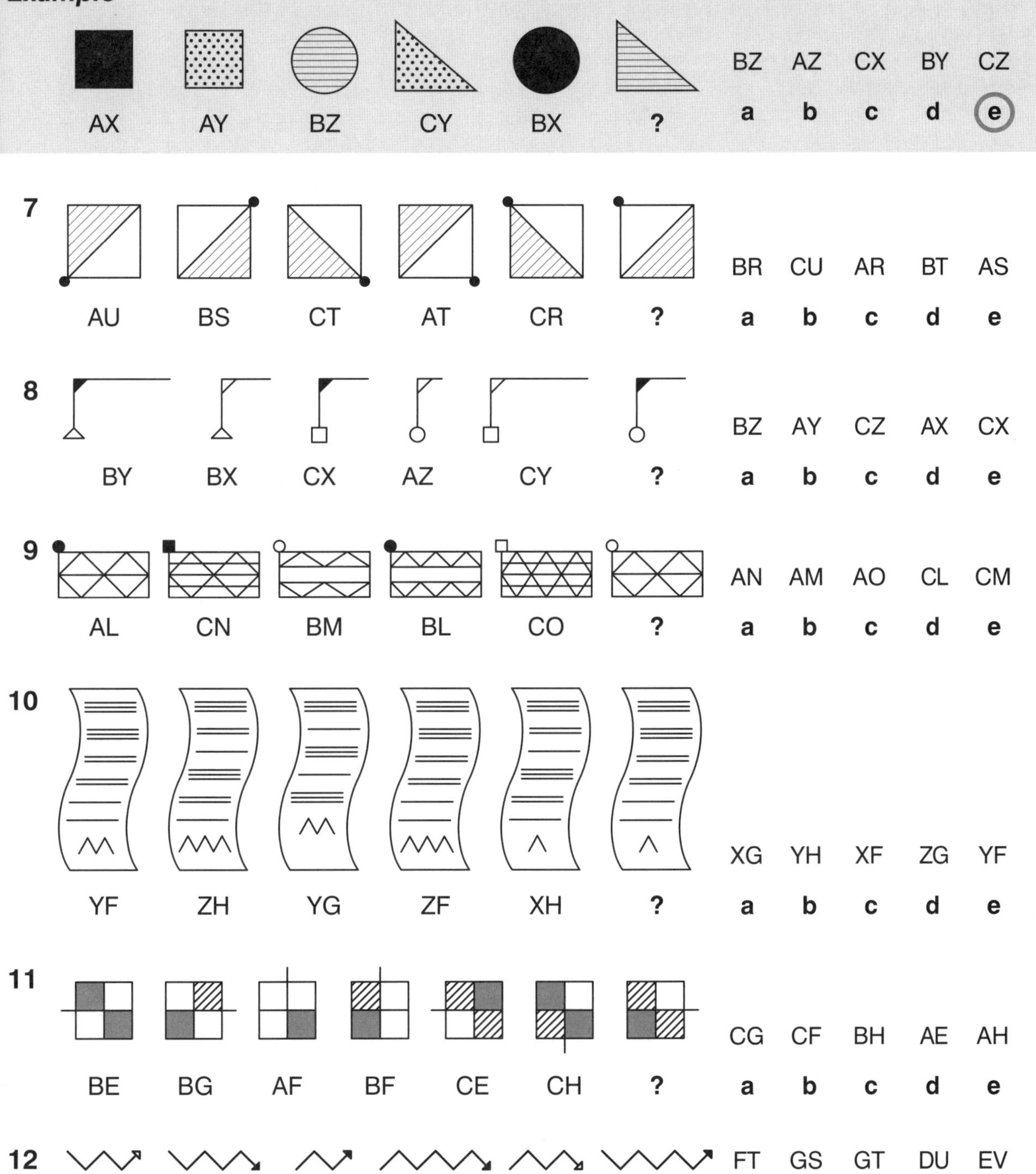

Time for a break! Go to Puzzle Page 42

Total

TEST 5: **Analogies and Cubes**

Test time: 0 5 10 minutes

Which shape or pattern on the right completes the second pair in the same way as the first pair?

Example

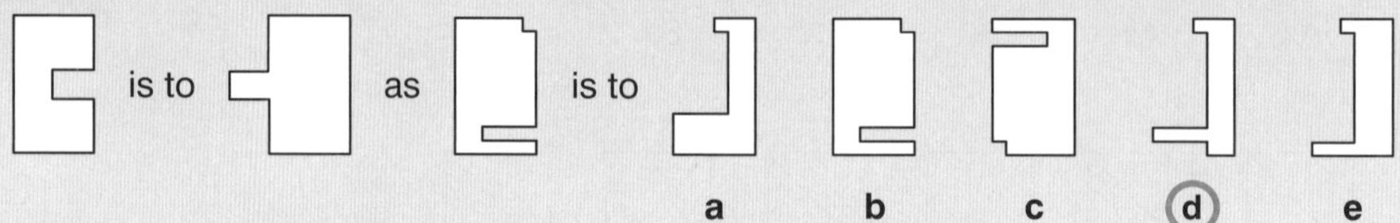

1

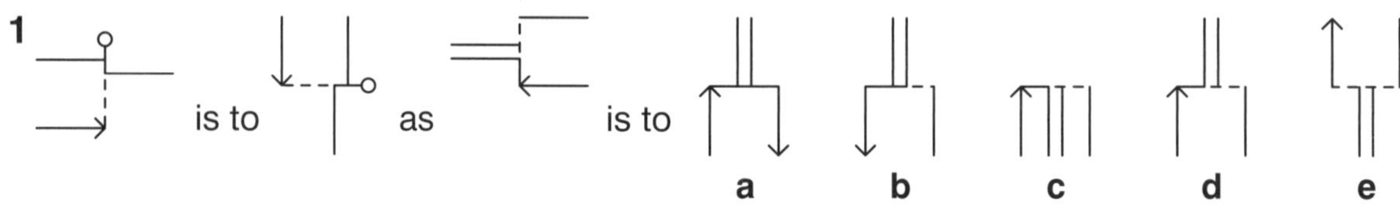

2

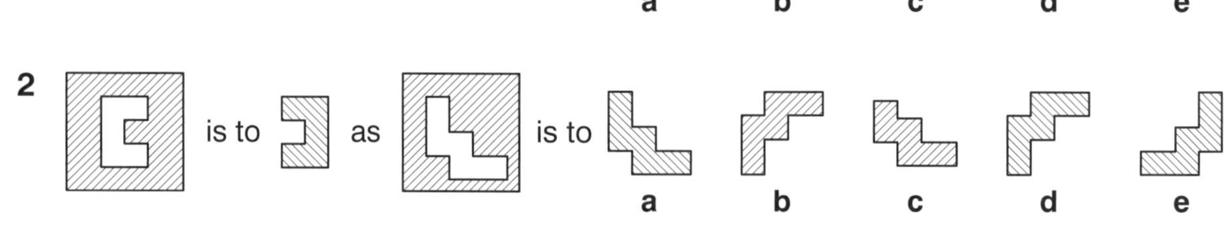

3

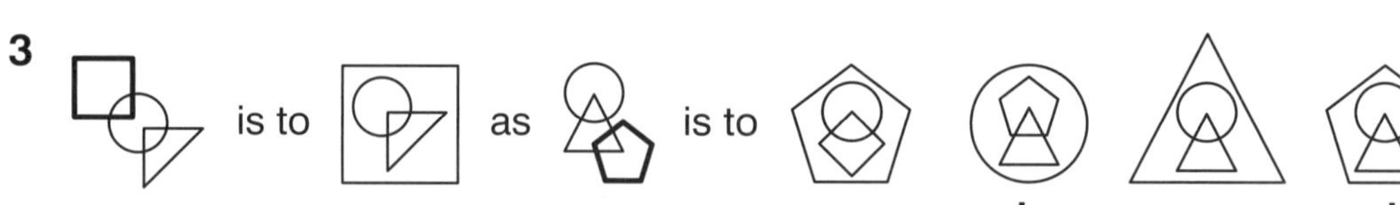

4

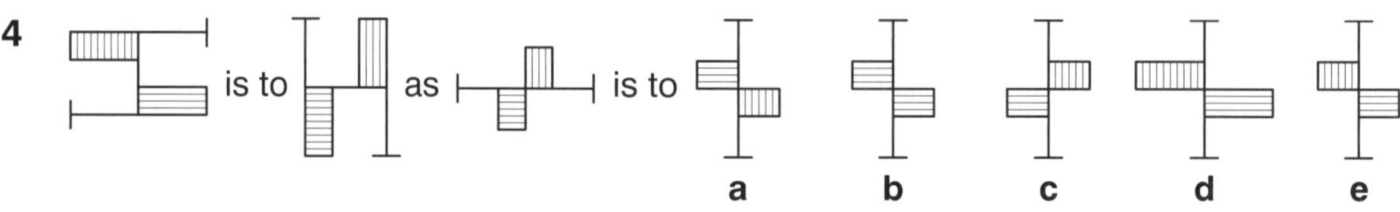

5

6

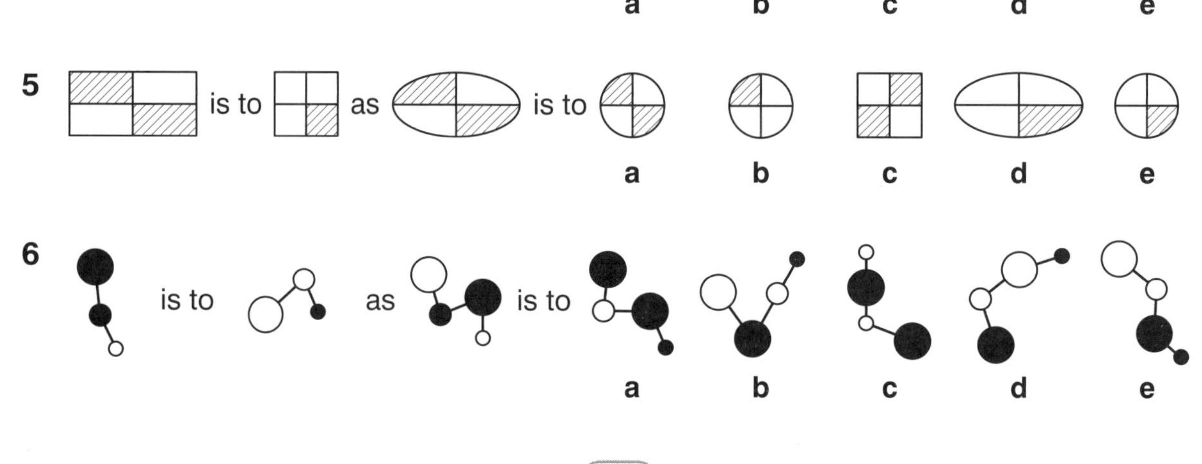

Which cube cannot be made from the given net?

Example

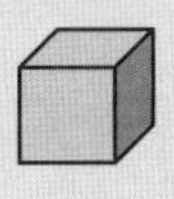
a

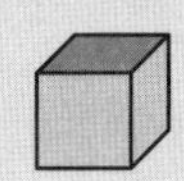
b

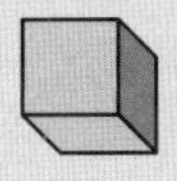
c

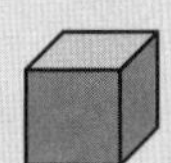
(d)

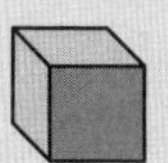
e

7

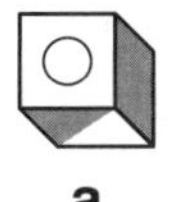
a

b

c

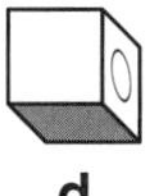
d

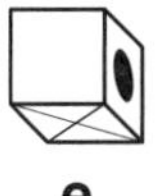
e

8

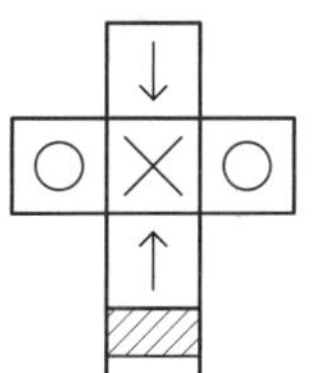

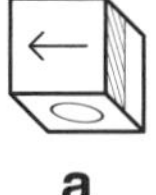
a

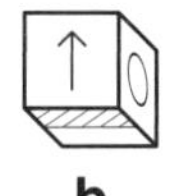
b

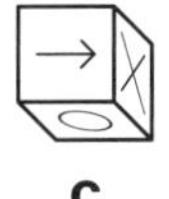
c

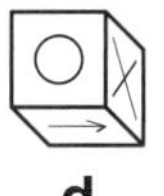
d

e

9

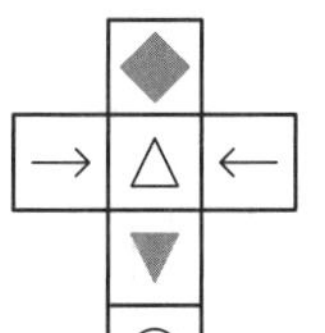

a

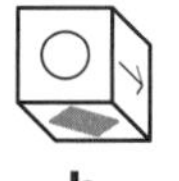
b

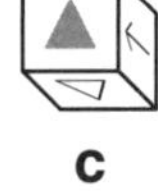
c

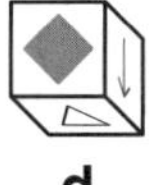
d

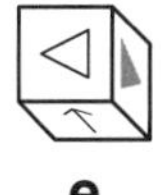
e

10

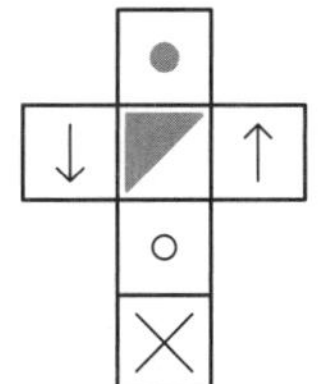

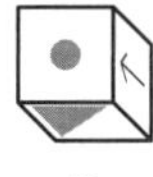
a

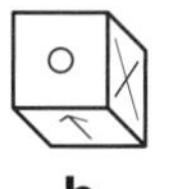
b

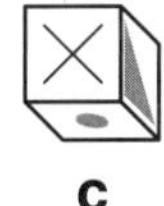
c

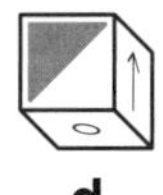
d

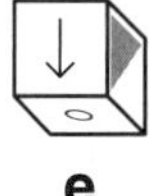
e

11

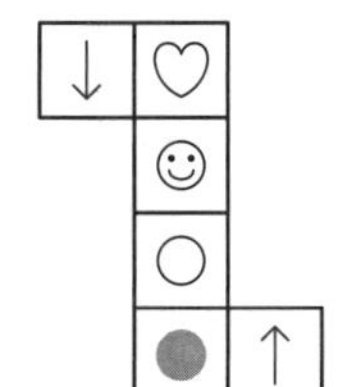

a

b

c

d

e

12

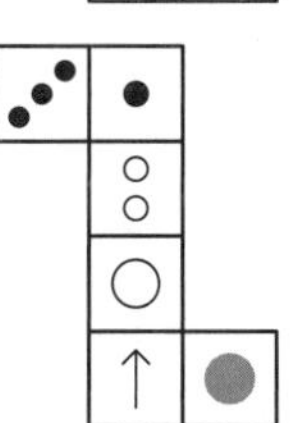

a

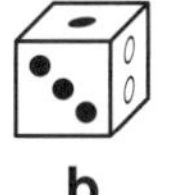
b

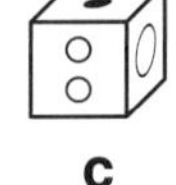
c

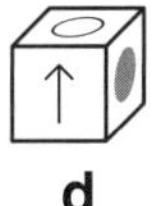
d

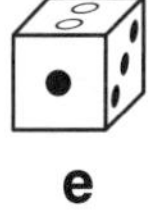
e

Total

TEST 6: Symmetry and Codes

Test time: 0 5 10 minutes

Which shape on the right is the reflection of the shape given on the left?

Example

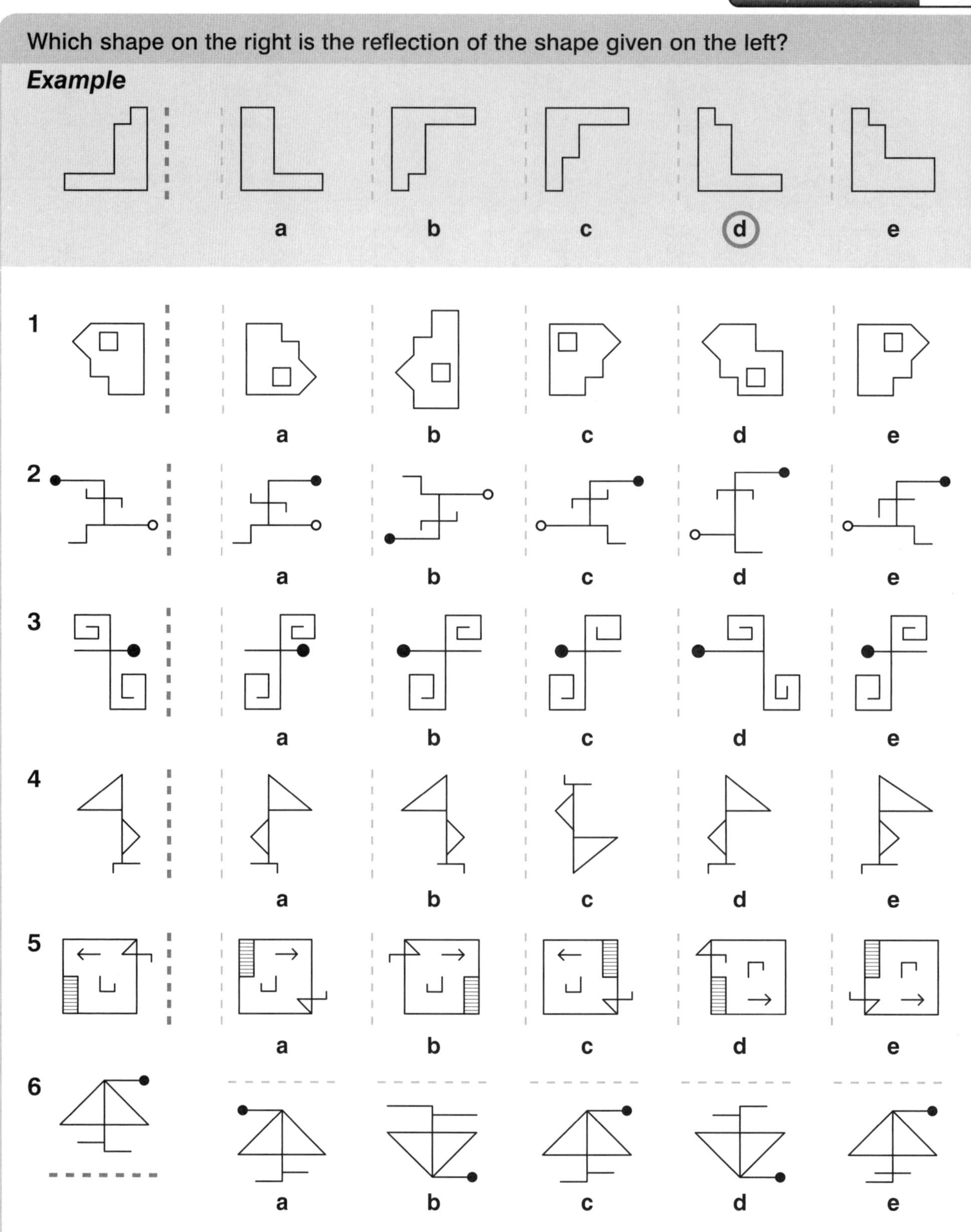

Which code matches the shape or pattern given at the end of each line?

Example

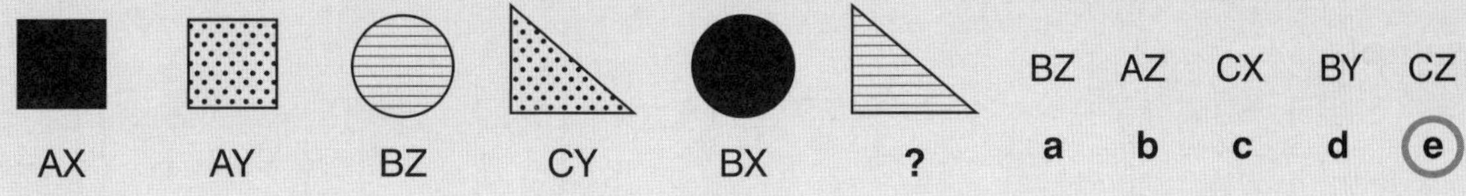

AX AY BZ CY BX ?

BZ	AZ	CX	BY	CZ
a	**b**	**c**	**d**	**e** (circled)

7

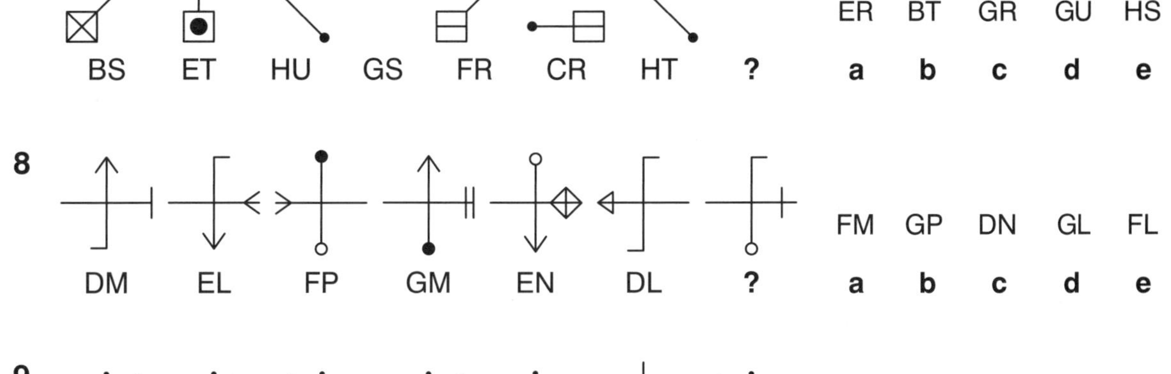

BS ET HU GS FR CR HT ?

ER	BT	GR	GU	HS
a	**b**	**c**	**d**	**e**

8

DM EL FP GM EN DL ?

FM	GP	DN	GL	FL
a	**b**	**c**	**d**	**e**

9

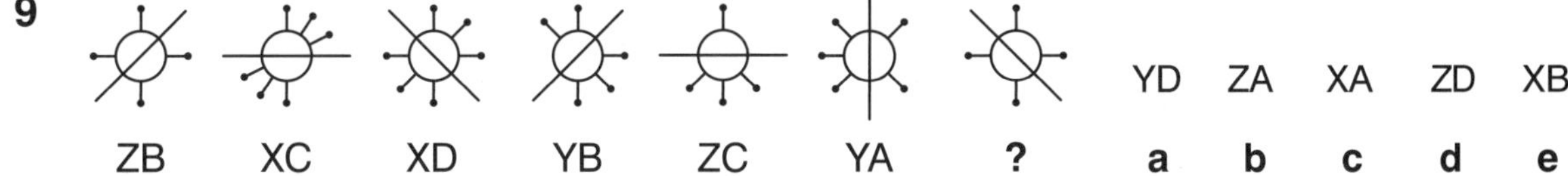

ZB XC XD YB ZC YA ?

YD	ZA	XA	ZD	XB
a	**b**	**c**	**d**	**e**

10

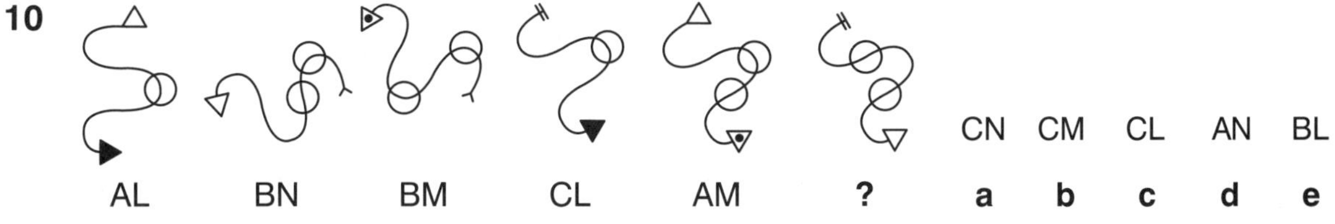

AL BN BM CL AM ?

CN	CM	CL	AN	BL
a	**b**	**c**	**d**	**e**

11

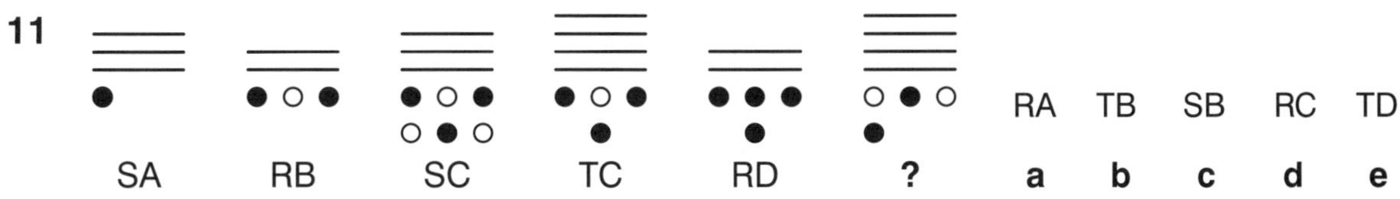

SA RB SC TC RD ?

RA	TB	SB	RC	TD
a	**b**	**c**	**d**	**e**

12

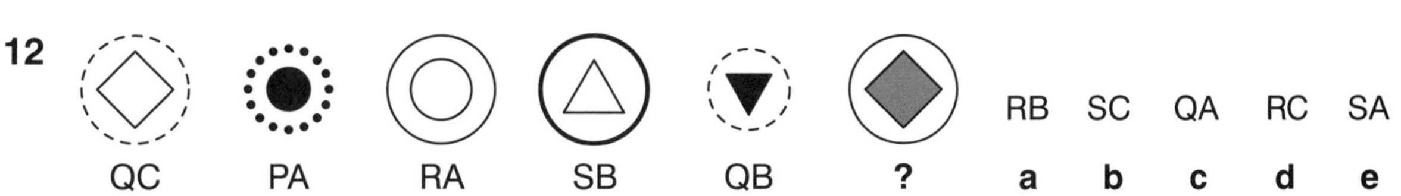

QC PA RA SB QB ?

RB	SC	QA	RC	SA
a	**b**	**c**	**d**	**e**

Total

TEST 7: Symmetry and Cubes

Test time: 0 5 10 minutes

Which shape on the right is the reflection of the shape given on the left?

Example

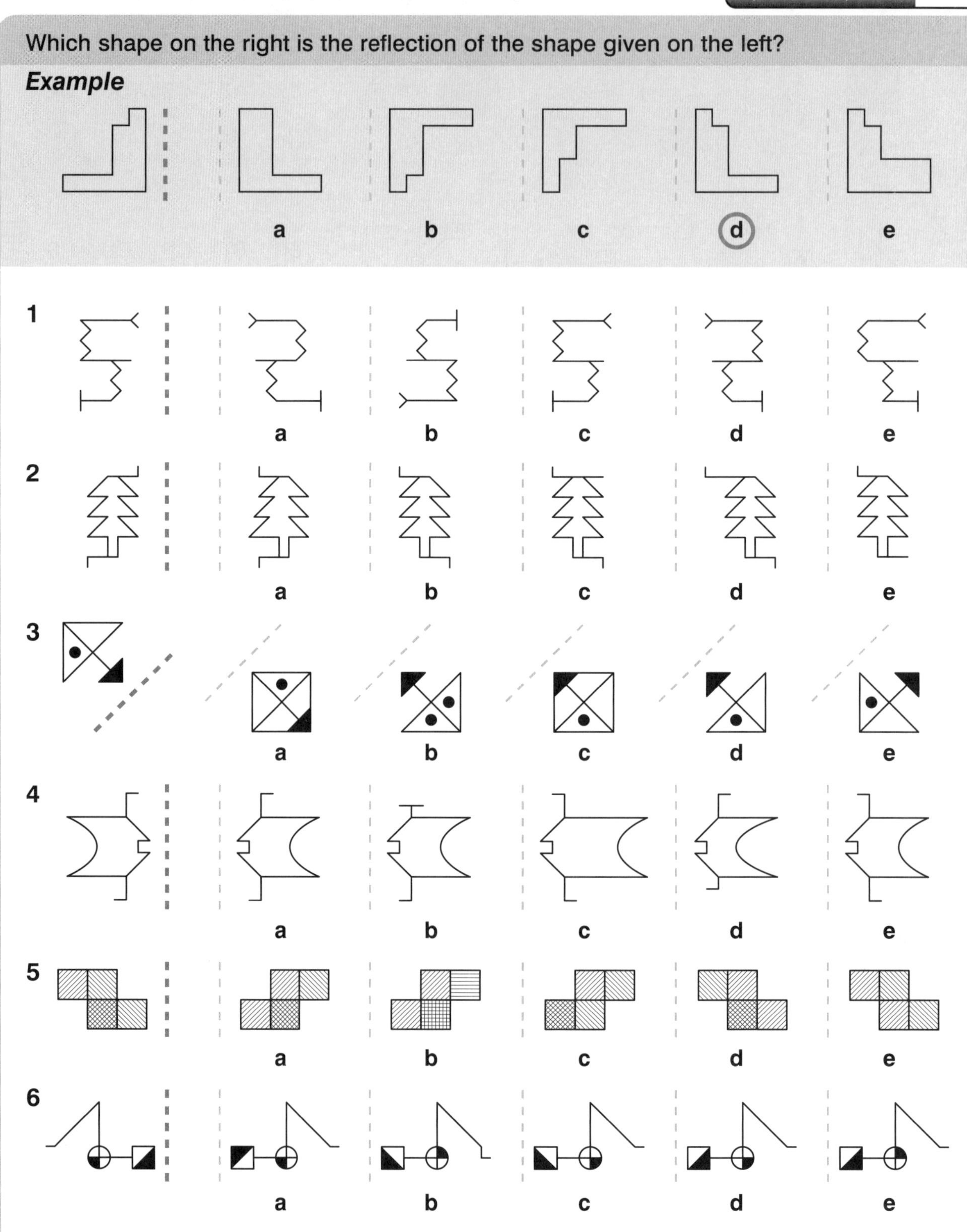

Which cube cannot be made from the given net?

Example

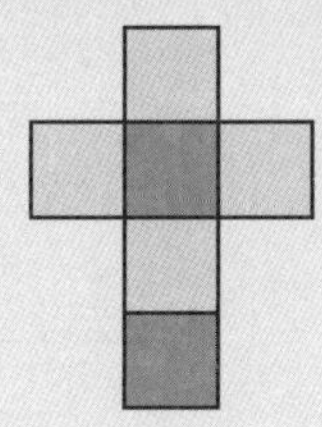

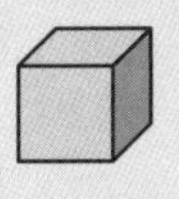
a

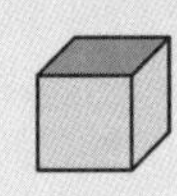
b

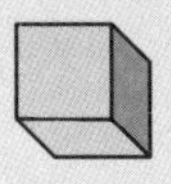
c

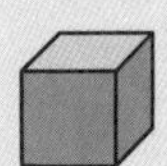
d

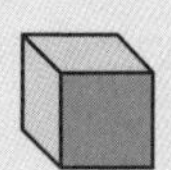
e

7

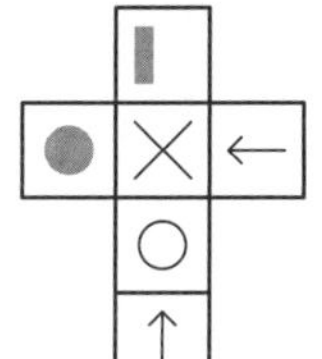

a

b

c

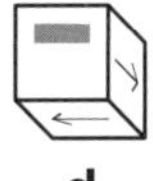
d

e

8

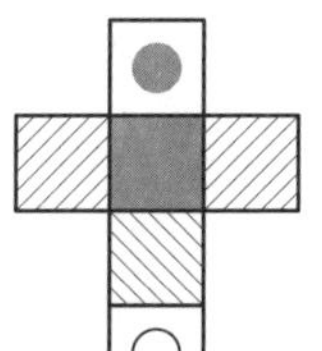

a

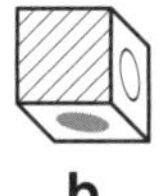
b

c

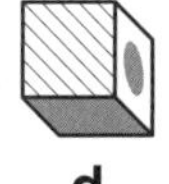
d

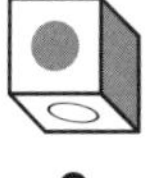
e

9

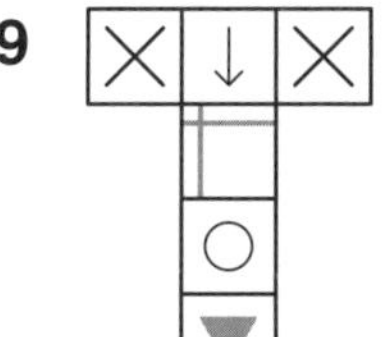

a

b

c

d

e

10

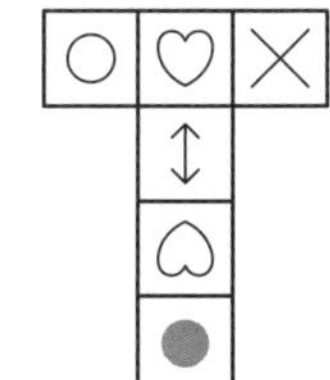

a

b

c

d

e

11

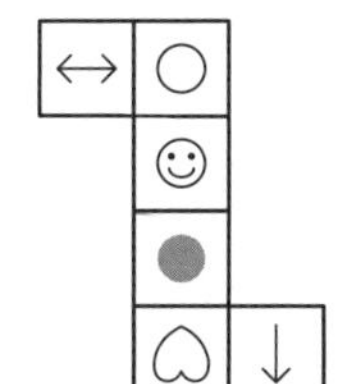

a

b

c

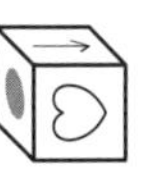
d

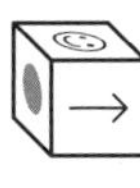
e

12

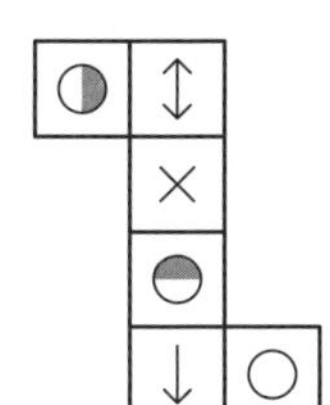

a

b

c

d

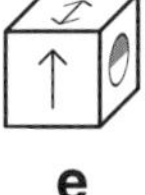
e

Total

TEST 8: **Similarities and Codes**

Test time: 0 5 10 minutes

Which pattern on the right belongs in the group on the left?

Example

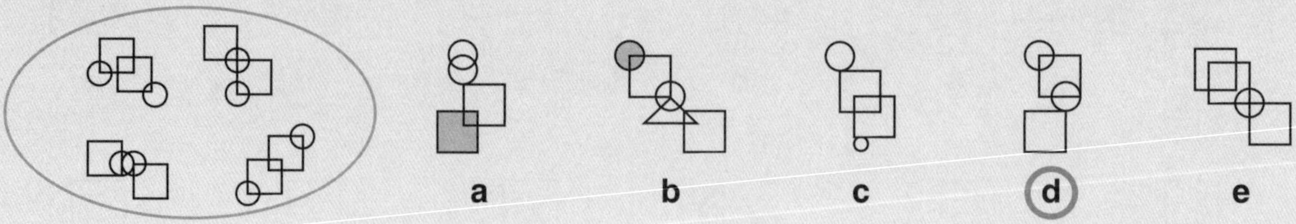

a b c (d) e

1

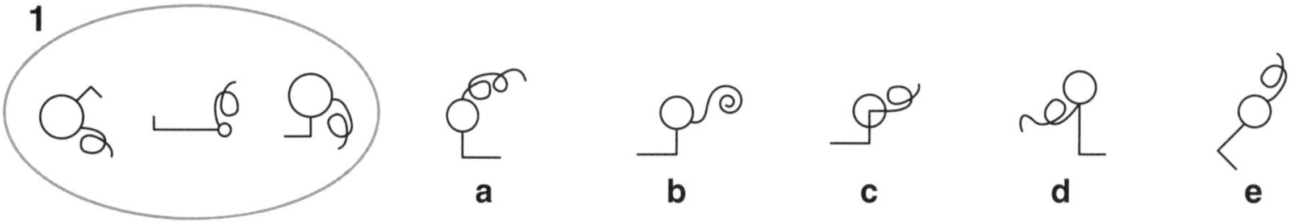

a b c d e

2

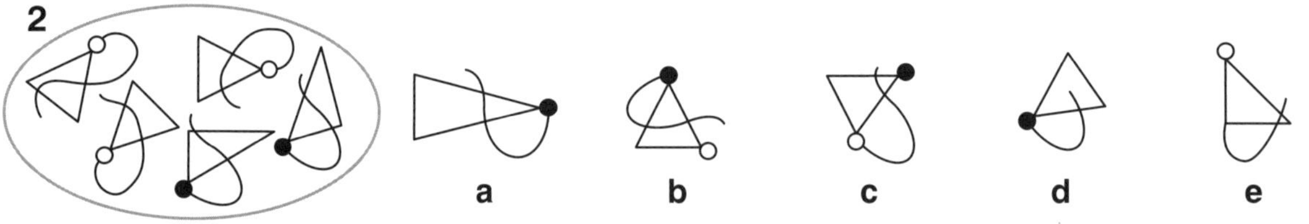

a b c d e

3

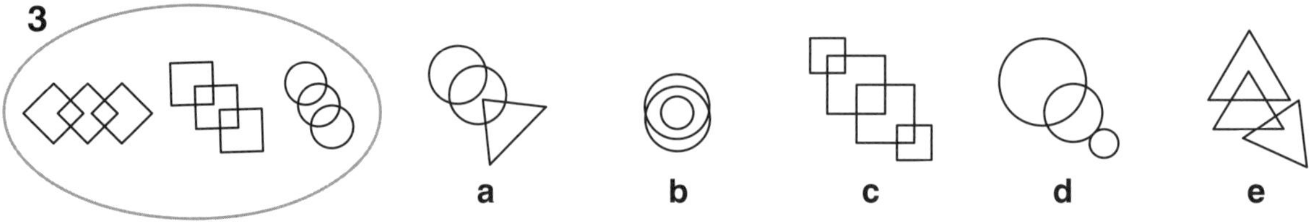

a b c d e

4

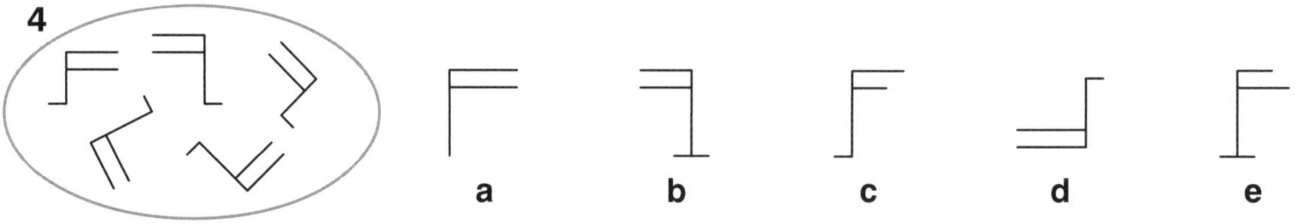

a b c d e

5

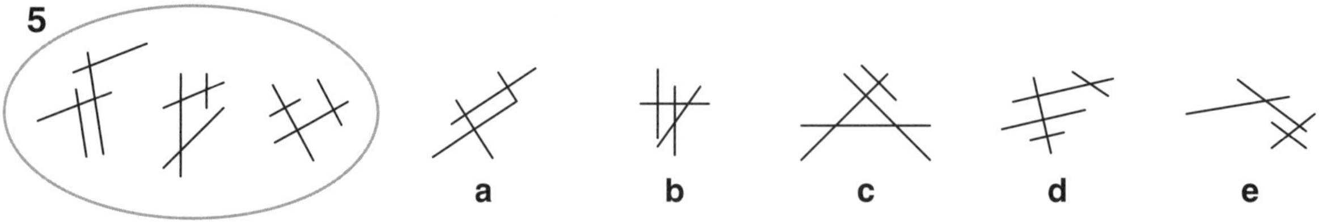

a b c d e

6

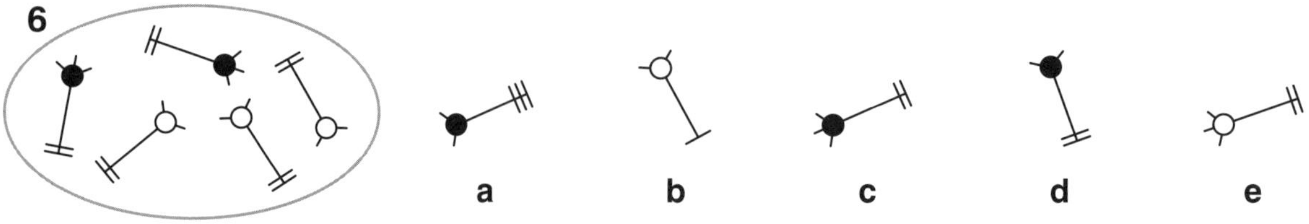

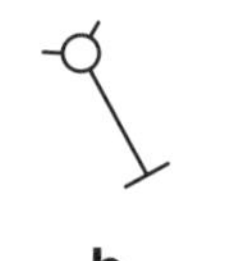

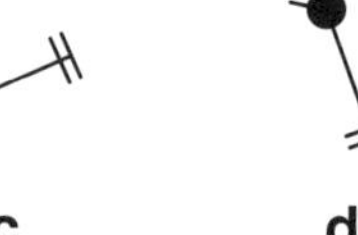

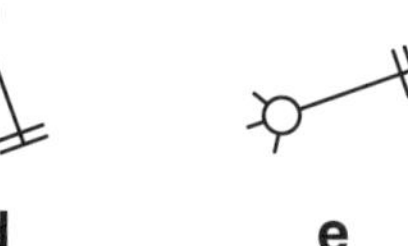

a b c d e

Which code matches the shape or pattern given at the end of each line?

Example

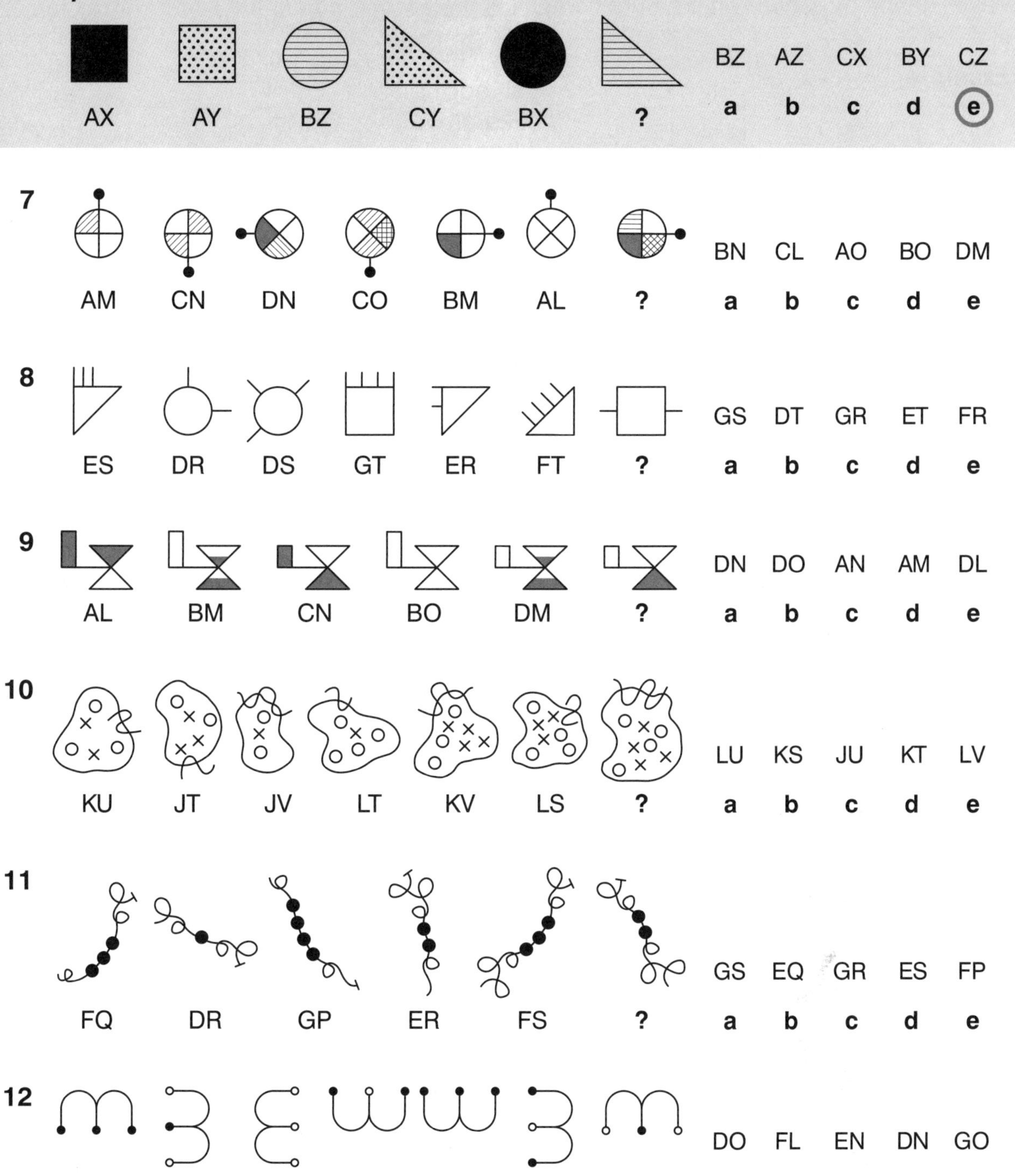

Test 9: Analogies and Sequences

Test time: 0 5 10 minutes

Which shape or pattern on the right completes the second pair in the same way as the first pair?

Example

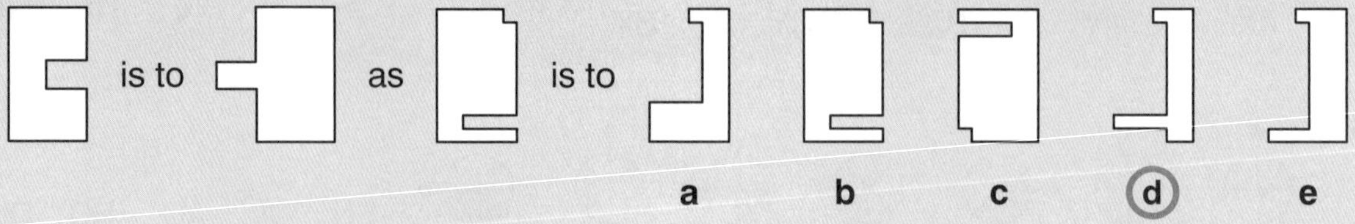

is to as is to

a b c (d) e

1 is to as is to

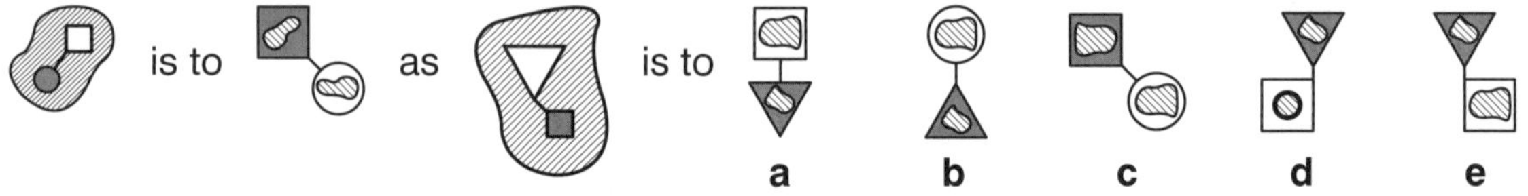

a b c d e

2 is to as is to

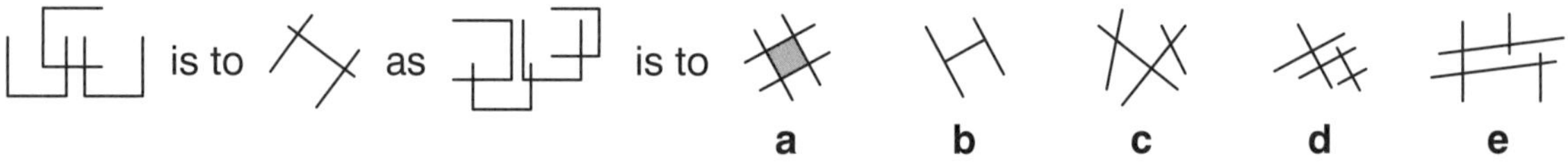

a b c d e

3 is to as is to

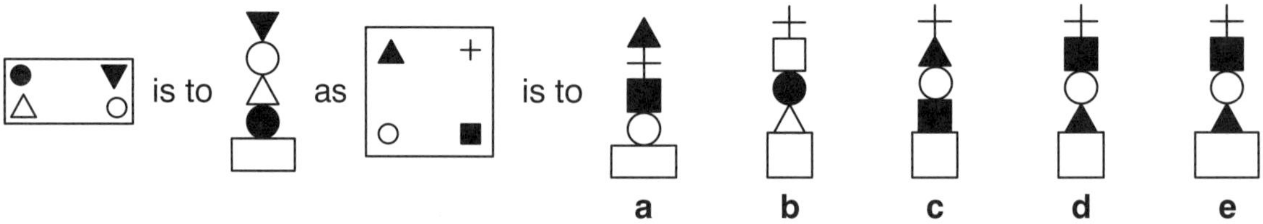

a b c d e

4 is to as is to

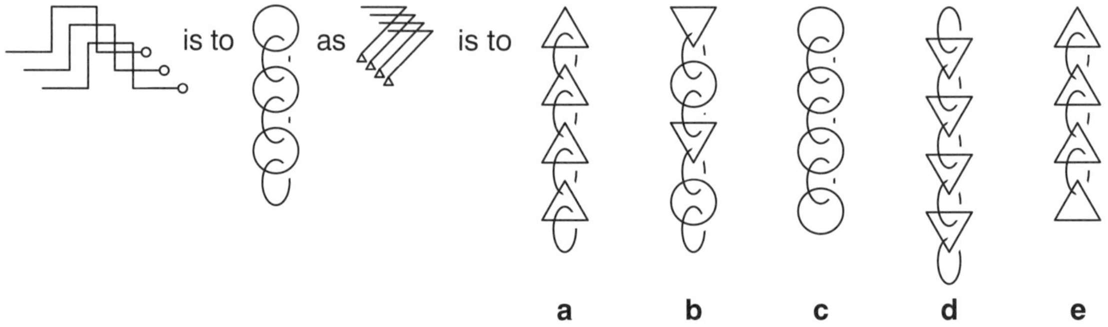

a b c d e

5 is to as is to

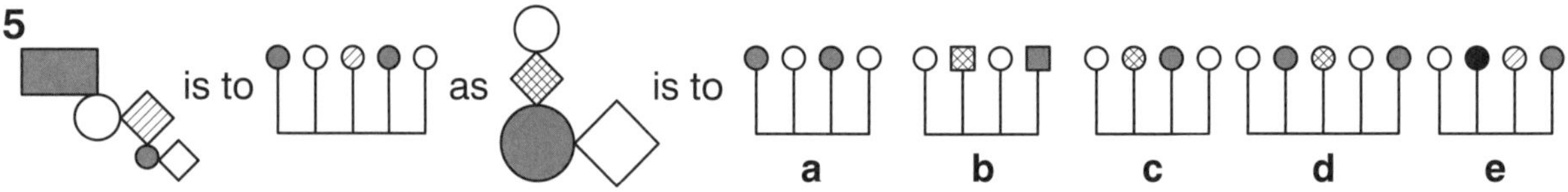

a b c d e

6 is to as is to

a b c d e

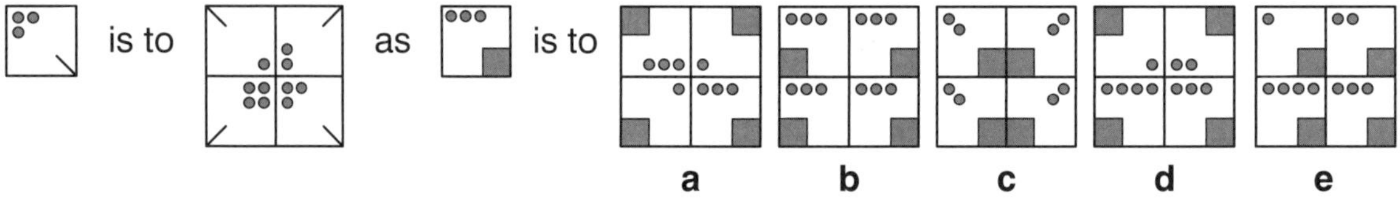

Which one comes next?

Example

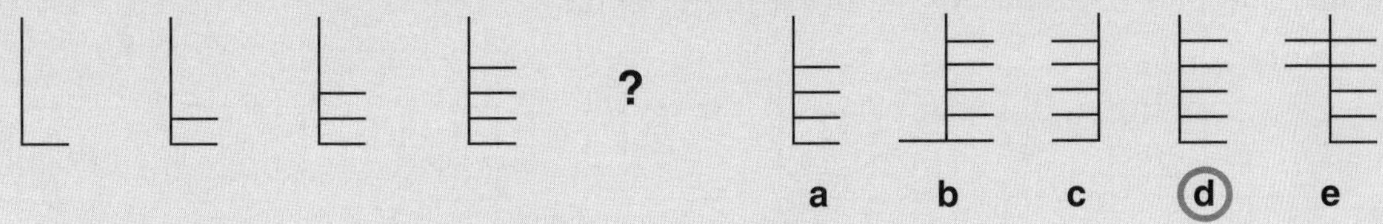

7 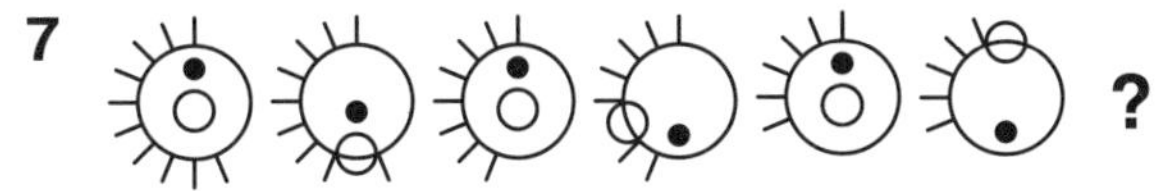 ?

8 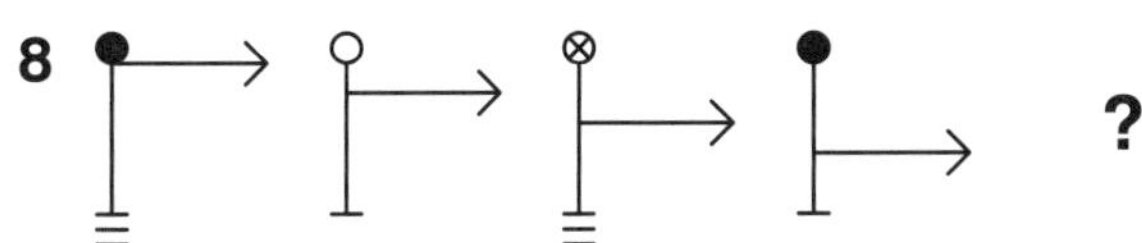 ?

9 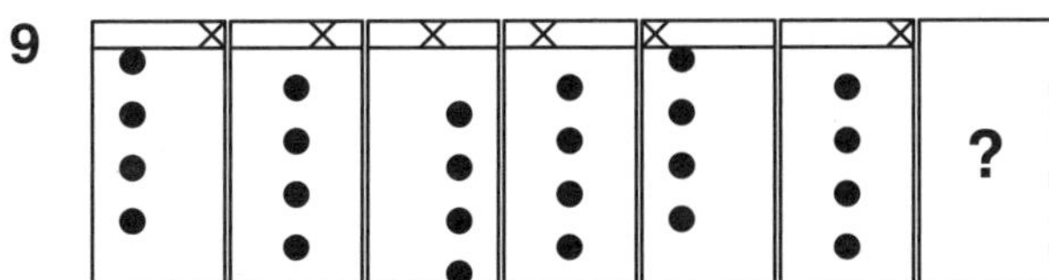 ?

10 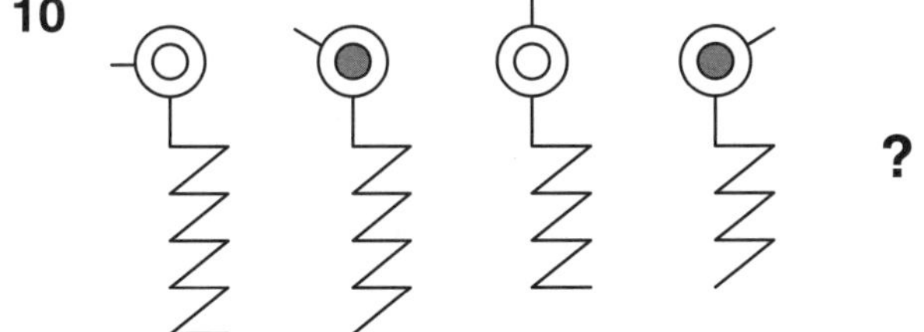 ?

11 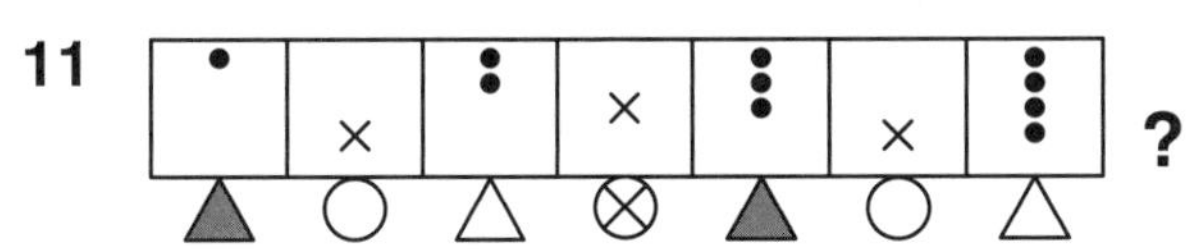 ?

12 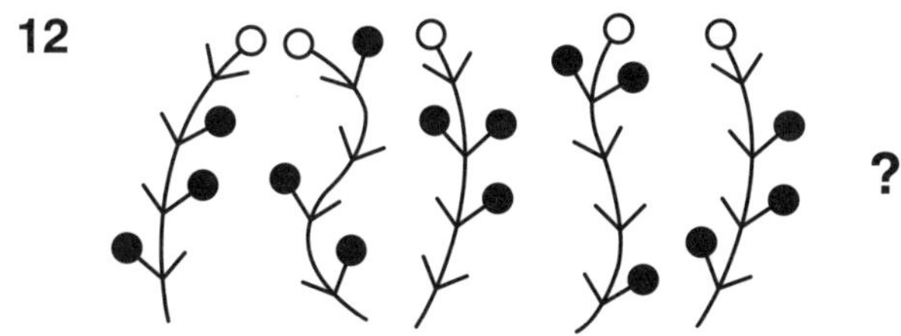 ?

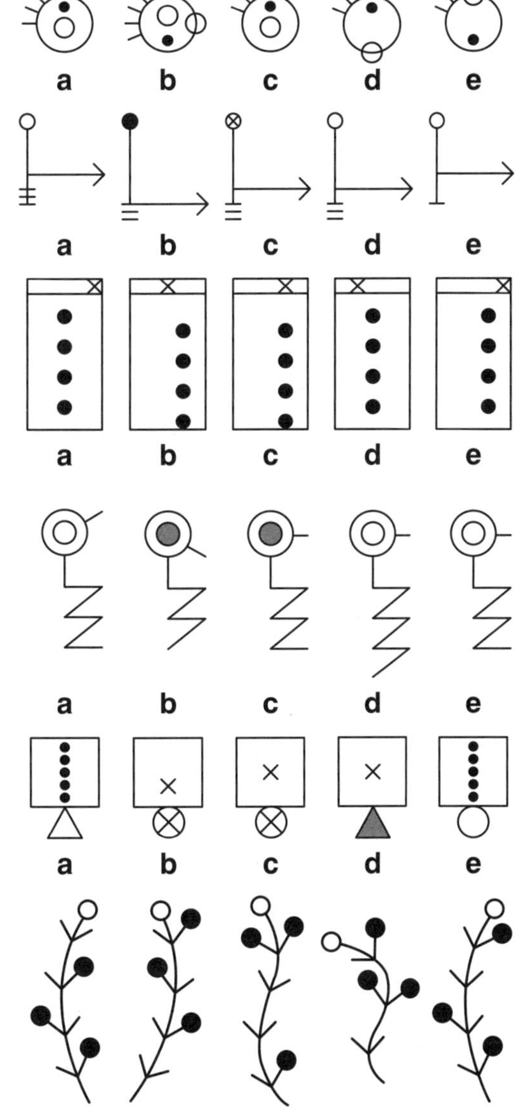

TEST 10: **Grids and Cubes**

Test time: 0 5 10 minutes

Which shape or pattern completes the larger square?

Example

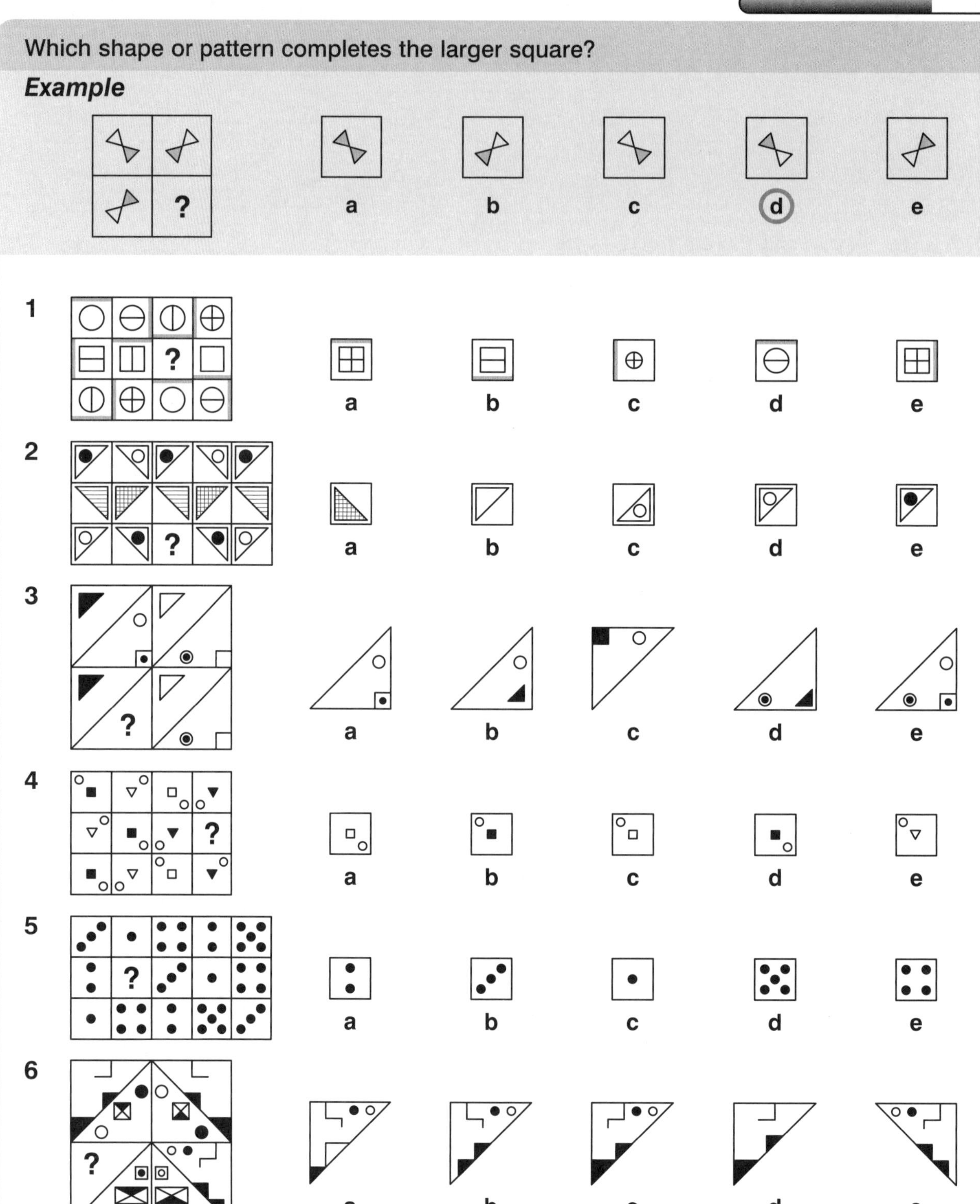

Which cube cannot be made from the given net?

Example

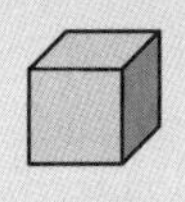
a

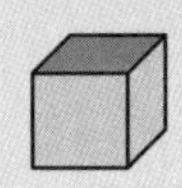
b

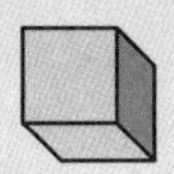
c

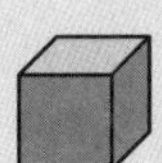
(d)

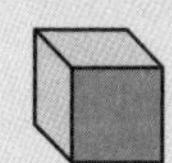
e

7

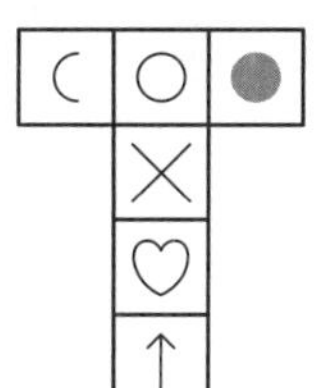

a

b

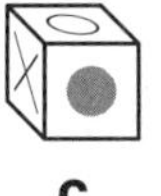
c

d

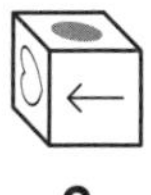
e

8

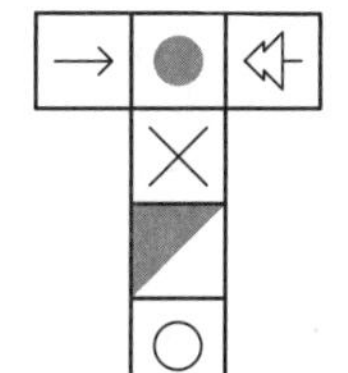

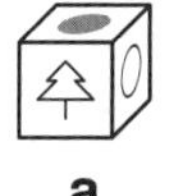
a

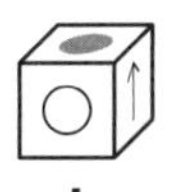
b

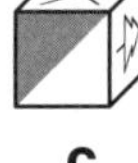
c

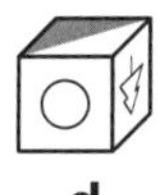
d

e

9

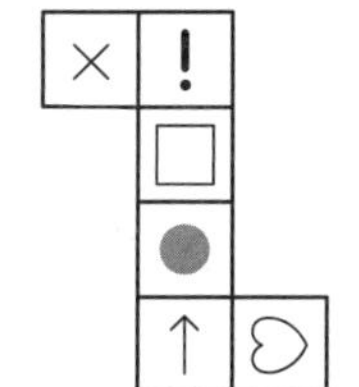

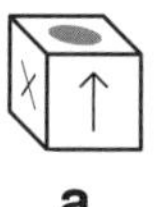
a

b

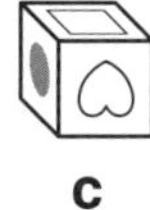
c

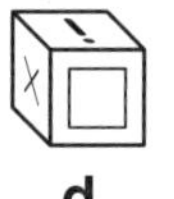
d

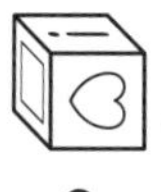
e

10

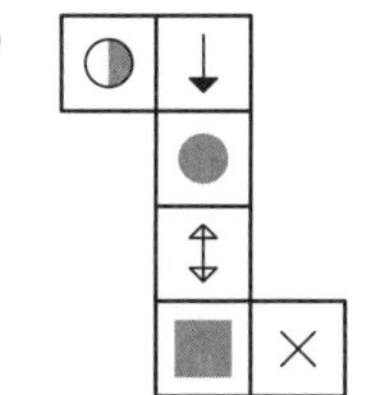

a

b

c

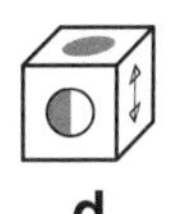
d

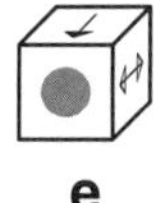
e

11

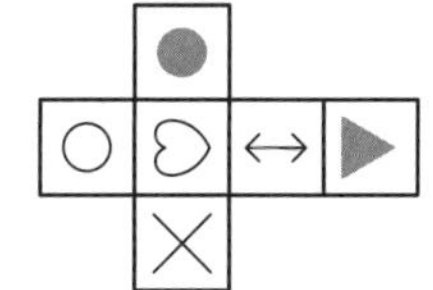

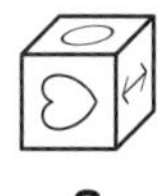
a

b

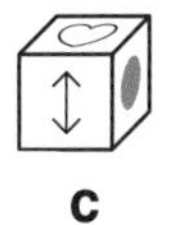
c

d

e

12

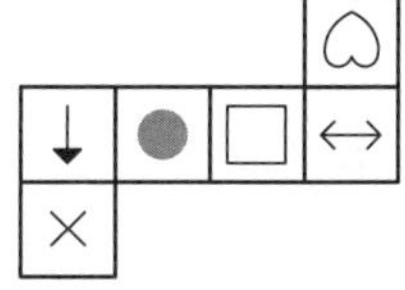

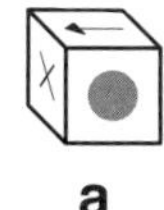
a

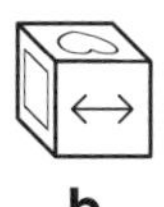
b

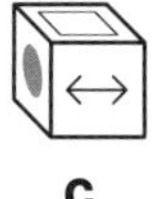
c

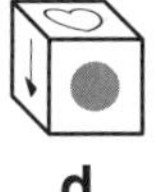
d

e

Total

Test 11: Mixed

Test time: 0 5 10 minu

Which shape or pattern on the right completes the second pair in the same way as the first pair?

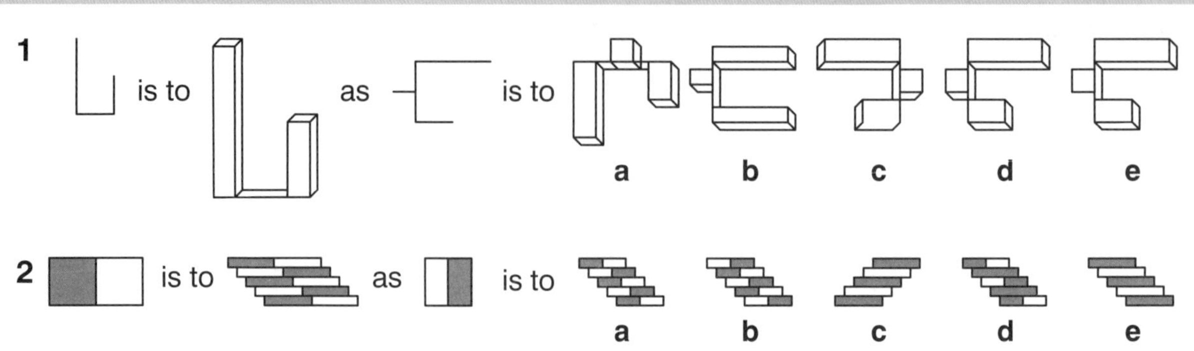

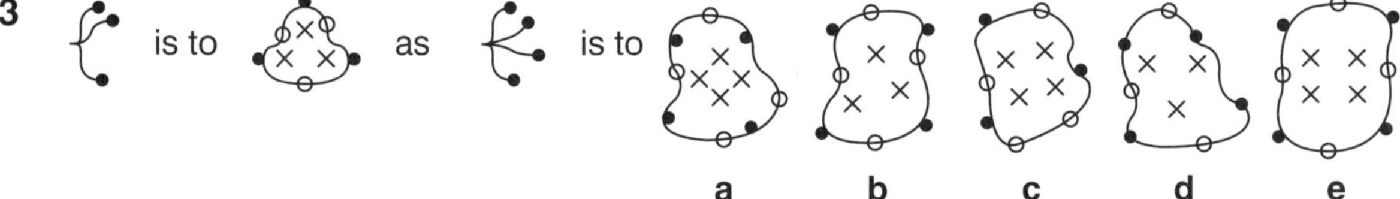

Which shape or pattern completes the larger square?

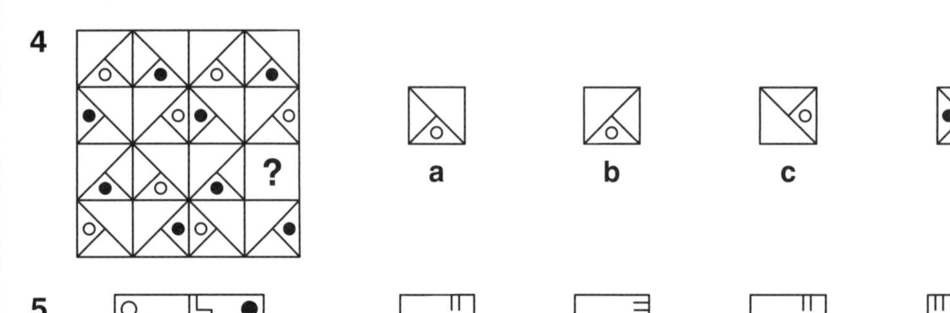

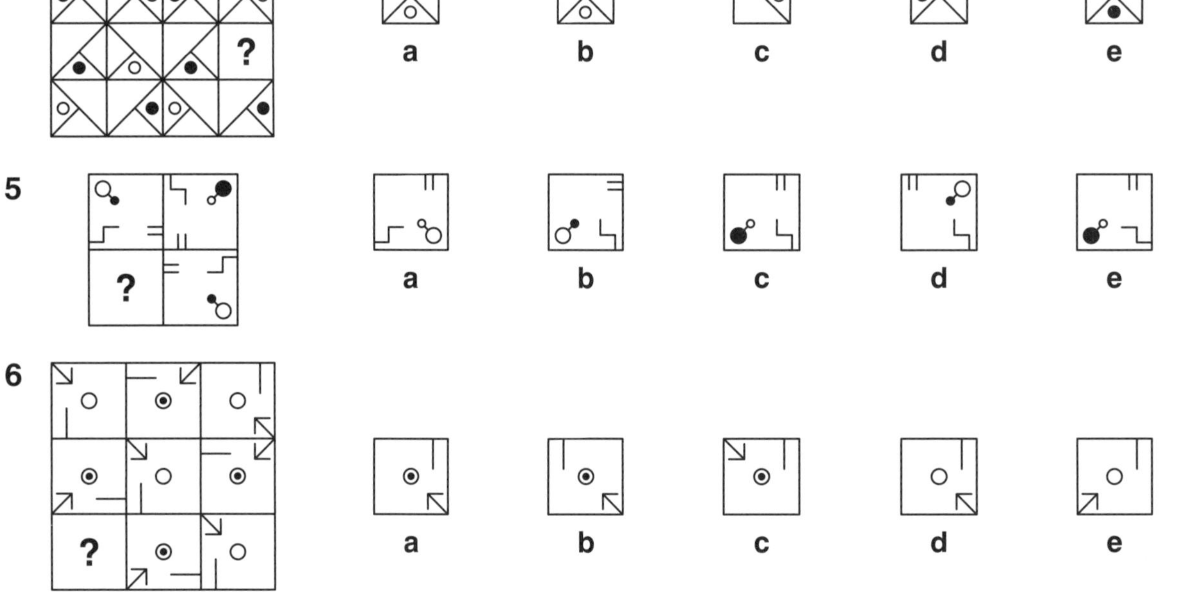

Which cube cannot be made from the given net?

7

a **b** **c** **d** **e**

8

a **b** **c** **d** **e**

9

a **b** **c** **d** **e**

Which code matches the shape or pattern given at the end of each line?

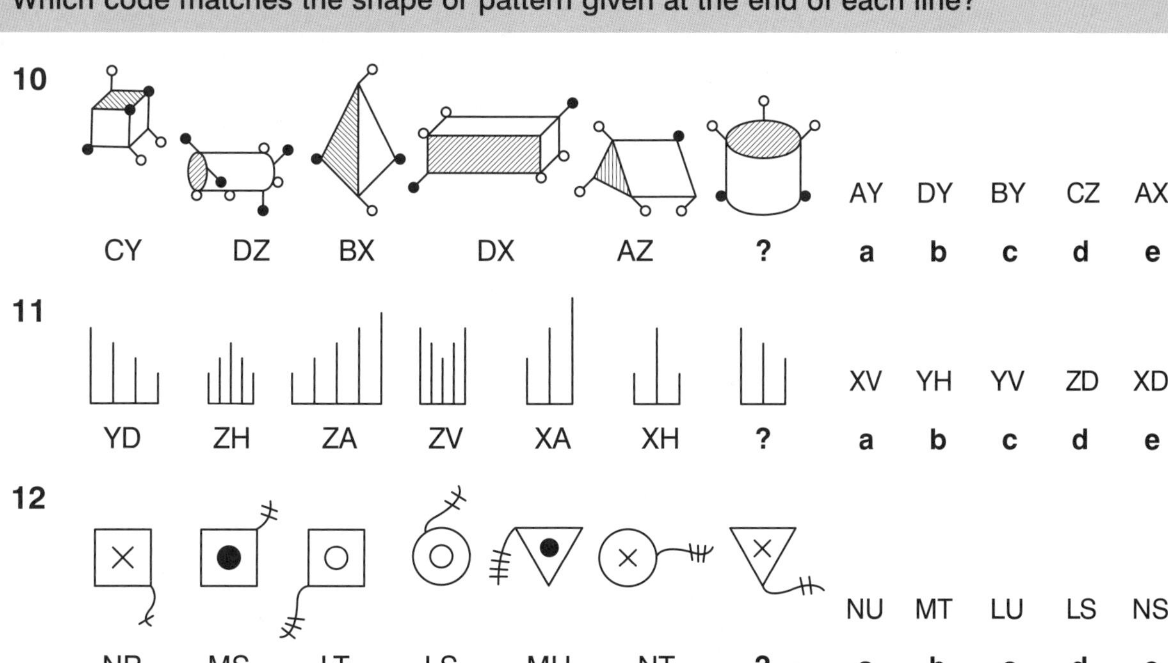

Total

Test 12: **Mixed**

Which pattern on the right belongs in the group on the left?

1

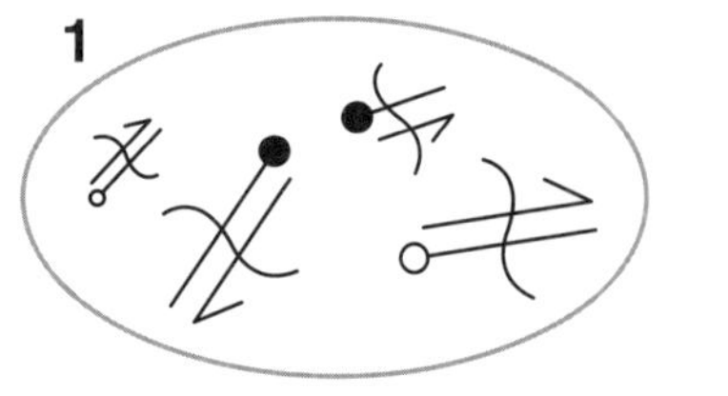

a

b

c

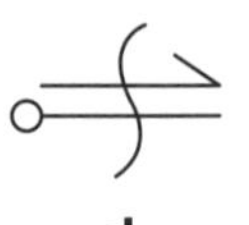
d

e

2

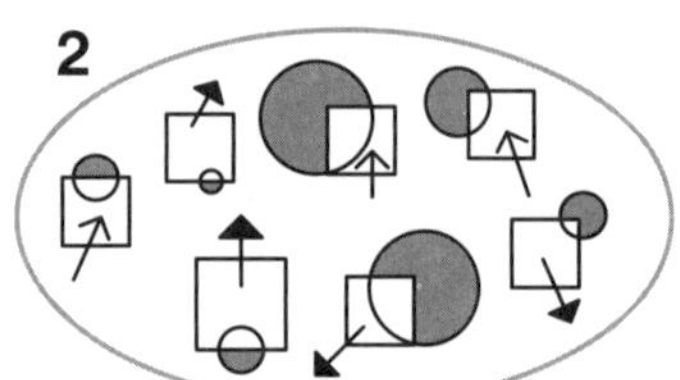

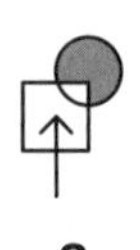
a

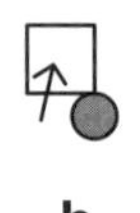
b

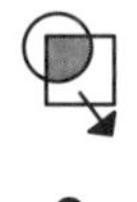
c

d

e

3

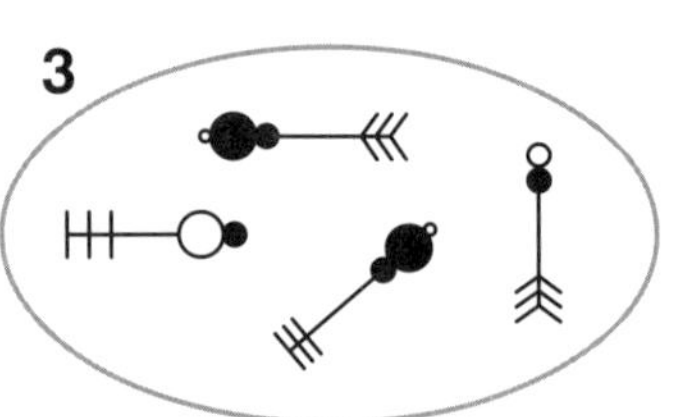

a

b

c

d

e

Which one comes next?

4

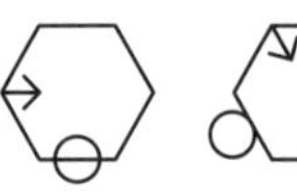

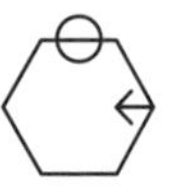
?

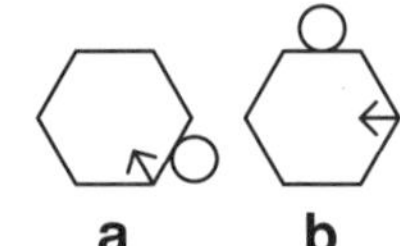
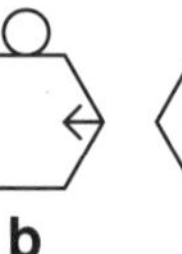
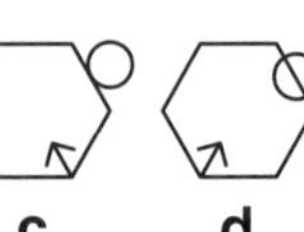
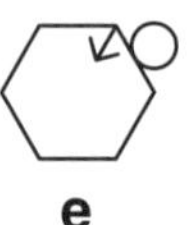

a **b** **c** **d** **e**

5

?

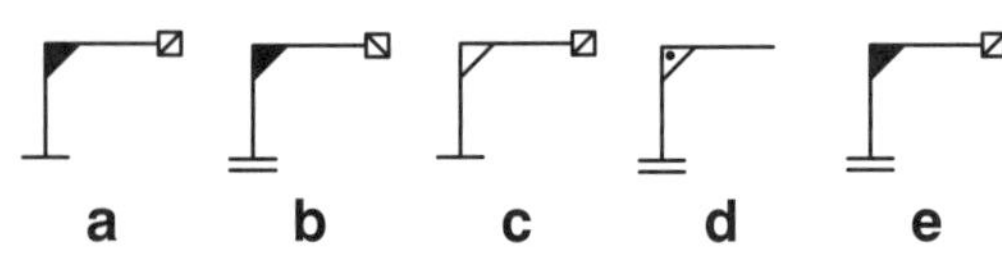

a **b** **c** **d** **e**

6

?

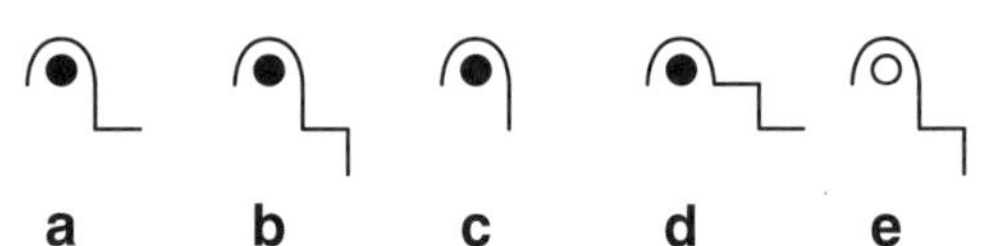

a **b** **c** **d** **e**

Answers

Test 1: Similarities and Grids

1	c
2	a
3	d
4	d
5	e
6	d
7	e
8	d
9	e
10	c
11	d
12	e

Test 2: Analogies and Reflection

1	e
2	e
3	c
4	d
5	e
6	b
7	c
8	e
9	d
10	e
11	d
12	c

Test 3: Sequences and Grids

1	e
2	c
3	e
4	d
5	d
6	a
7	c
8	e
9	d
10	d
11	c
12	d

Test 4: Similarities and Codes

1	e
2	b
3	d
4	e
5	e
6	c
7	a
8	d
9	b
10	c
11	a
12	c

Test 5: Analogies and Cubes

1	d
2	e
3	d
4	a
5	e
6	d
7	d
8	e
9	c
10	c
11	e
12	c

Test 6: Symmetry and Codes

1	e
2	c
3	e
4	a
5	b
6	d
7	c
8	e
9	d
10	a
11	b
12	d

Test 7: Symmetry and Cubes

1	d
2	b
3	d
4	e
5	a
6	c
7	c
8	e
9	d
10	c
11	d
12	b

Test 8: Similarities and Codes

1	e
2	a
3	e
4	d
5	e
6	c
7	d
8	c
9	a
10	e
11	d
12	d

Test 9: Analogies and Sequences

1	e
2	c
3	d
4	a
5	c
6	d
7	c
8	d
9	c
10	e
11	c
12	e

Answers

Test 10: Grids and Cubes

1 e
2 d
3 a
4 c
5 d
6 b
7 d
8 e
9 b
10 e
11 a
12 c

Test 11: Mixed

1 d
2 b
3 e
4 a
5 c
6 d
7 e
8 d
9 e
10 c
11 e
12 e

Test 12: Mixed

1 d
2 a
3 d
4 c
5 e
6 b
7 c
8 e
9 a
10 d
11 b
12 c

Test 13: Mixed

1 e
2 d
3 c
4 e
5 b
6 d
7 b
8 a
9 b
10 c
11 d
12 e

Test 14: Mixed

1 a
2 d
3 b
4 a
5 e
6 c
7 e
8 c
9 d
10 b
11 a
12 c

Test 15: Mixed

1 e
2 d
3 d
4 b
5 a
6 c
7 d
8 c
9 b
10 d
11 a
12 c

Test 16: Mixed

1 c
2 d
3 b
4 e
5 c
6 e
7 c
8 b
9 a
10 c
11 c
12 e

Test 17: Mixed

1 d
2 d
3 a
4 b
5 e
6 b
7 d
8 e
9 b
10 d
11 e
12 c

Test 18: Mixed

1 b
2 e
3 a
4 c
5 b
6 d
7 e
8 c
9 d
10 e
11 d
12 b

Answers

Test 19: Mixed

1 e
2 b
3 c
4 a
5 b
6 e
7 d
8 c
9 a
10 d
11 c
12 b

Test 20: Mixed

1 a
2 c
3 d
4 e
5 b
6 d
7 c
8 b
9 d
10 a
11 c
12 e

Answers

Puzzle 1

a 3
b 5
c 4
d 2
e 1

a 7
b 6
c 2
d 1
e 3
f 4
g 5

Puzzle 2

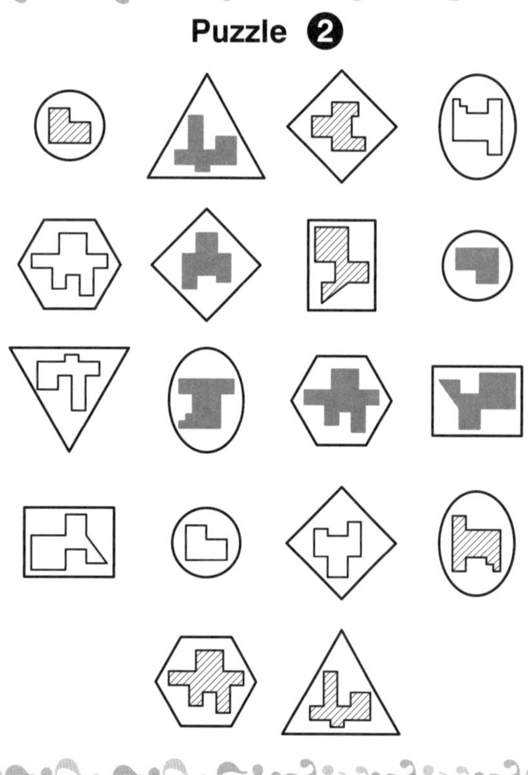

Puzzle 3

Puzzle 4

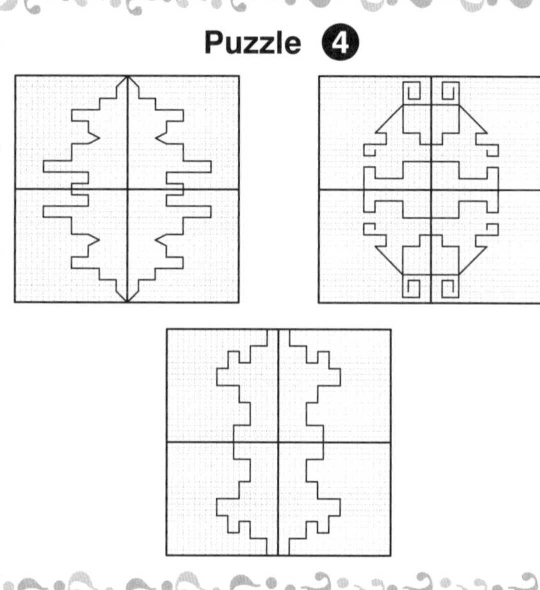

Puzzle 5

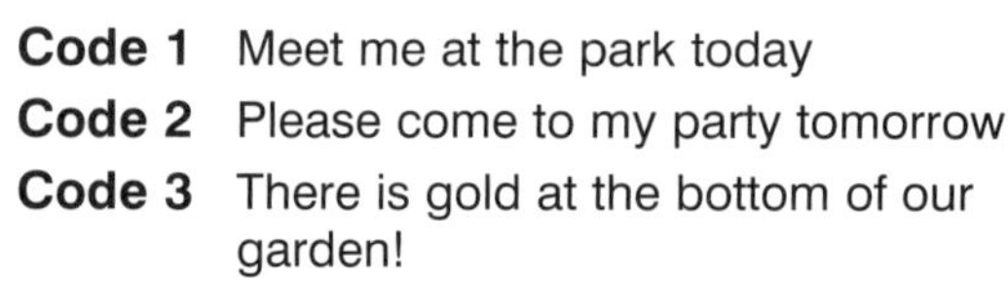

Code 1 Meet me at the park today
Code 2 Please come to my party tomorrow
Code 3 There is gold at the bottom of our garden!

Which cube cannot be made from the given net?

7

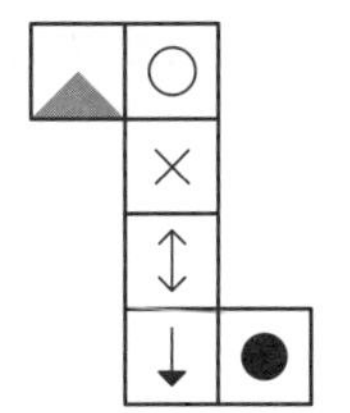

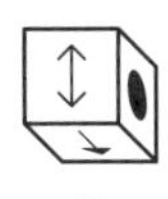
a

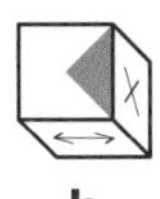
b

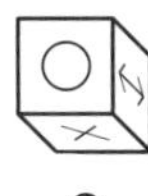
c

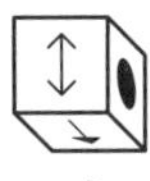
d

e

8

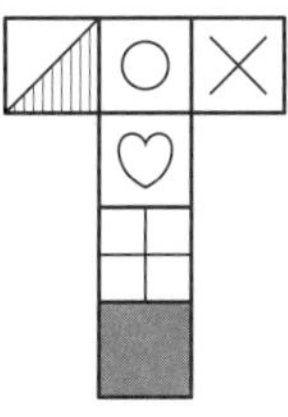

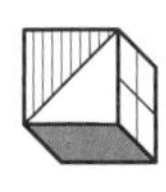
a

b

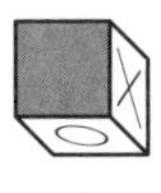
c

d

e

9

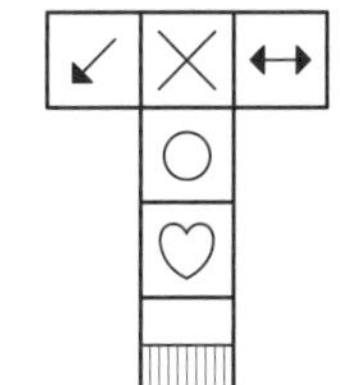

a

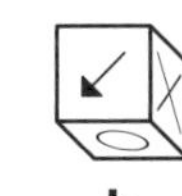
b

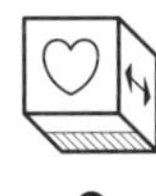
c

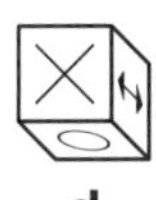
d

e

Which code matches the shape or pattern given at the end of each line?

10

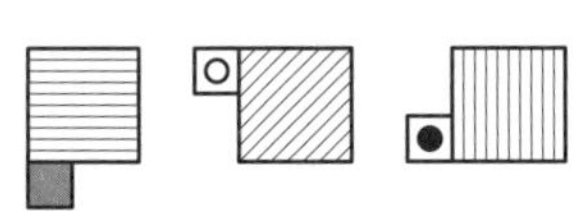

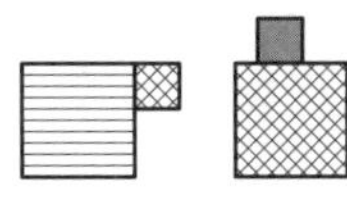
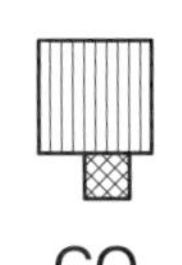
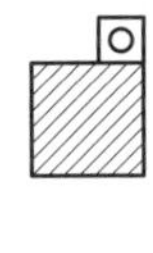

CP	DR	DS	BQ	AP	CQ	?

AS	CR	BP	AR	CS
a	**b**	**c**	**d**	**e**

11

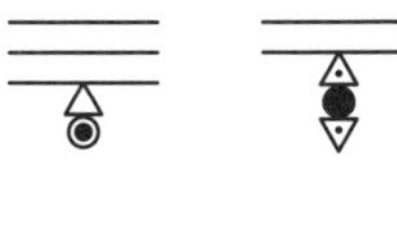
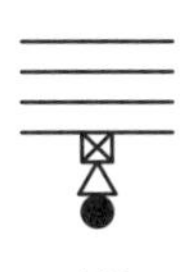
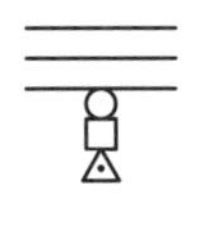

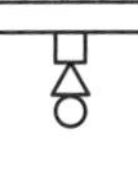

FB	HC	JC	FA	GB	?

HB	HA	JA	JB	FC
a	**b**	**c**	**d**	**e**

12

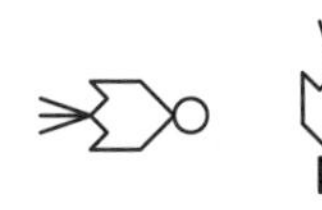

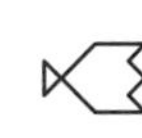
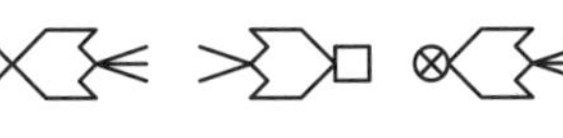
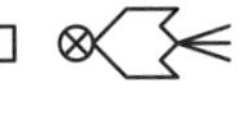

EA	SB	NA	SC	WC	EB	?

WB	EC	WA	SA	NB
a	**b**	**c**	**d**	**e**

Time for a break! Go to Puzzle Page 44

Total

TEST 13: **Mixed**

Test time: 0 5 10 minutes

Which shape or pattern on the right completes the second pair in the same way as the first pair?

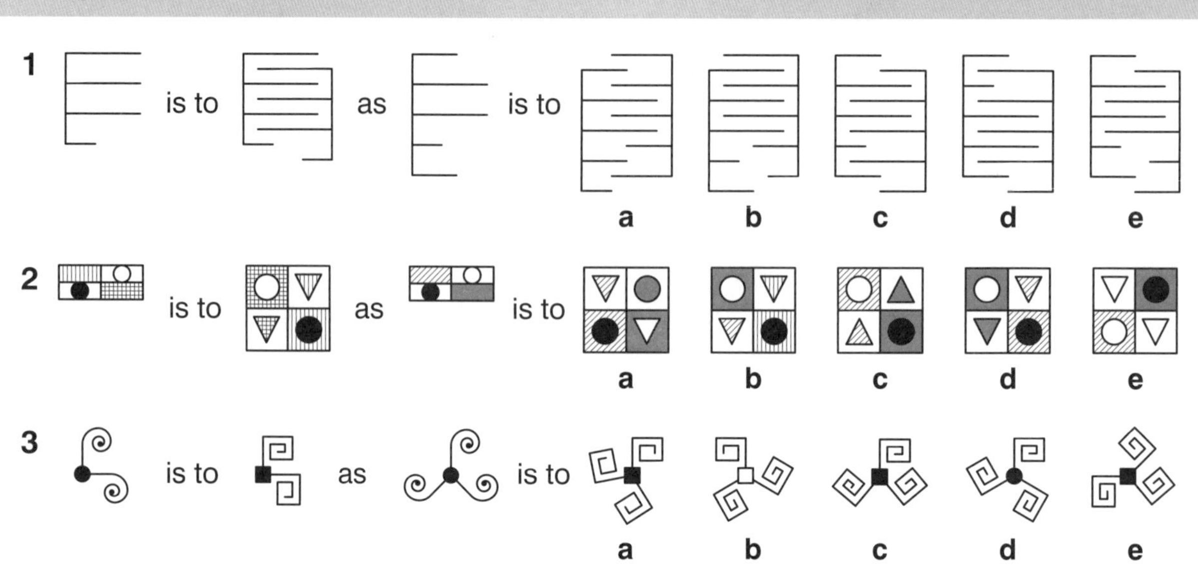

Which shape on the right is the reflection of the shape given on the left?

4

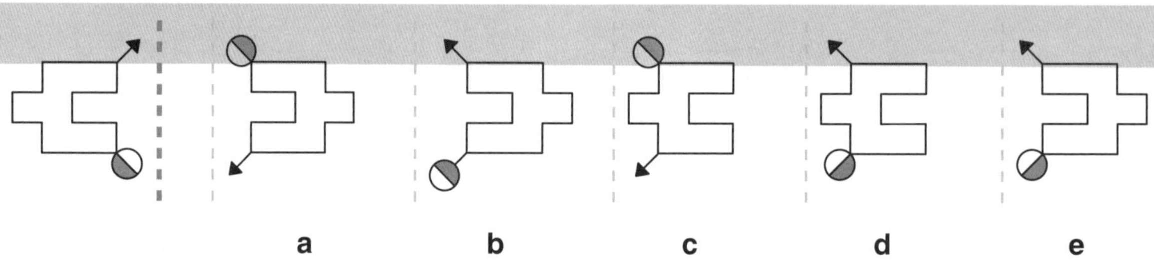

a b c d e

5

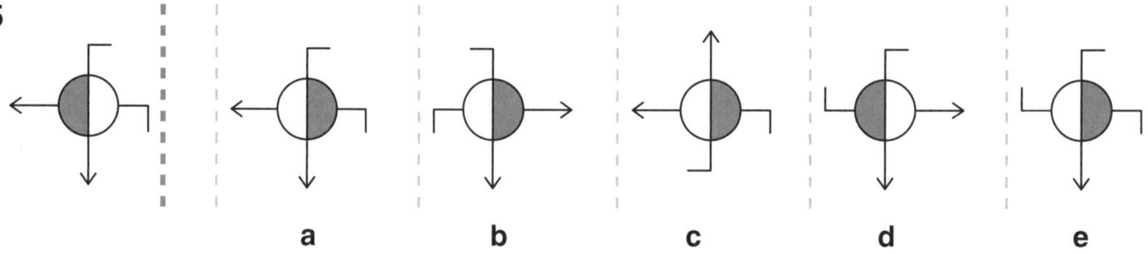

a b c d e

6

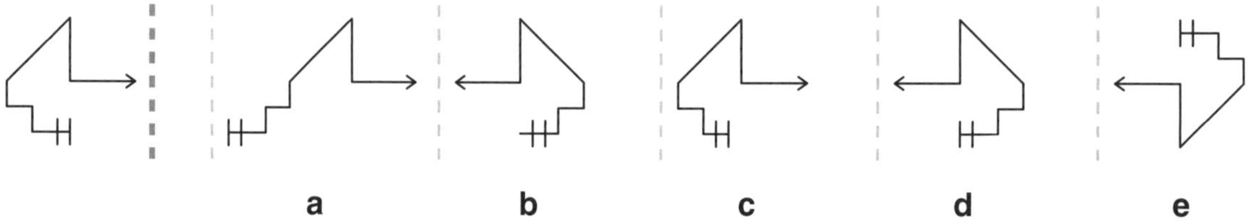

a b c d e

Which code matches the shape or pattern given at the end of each line?

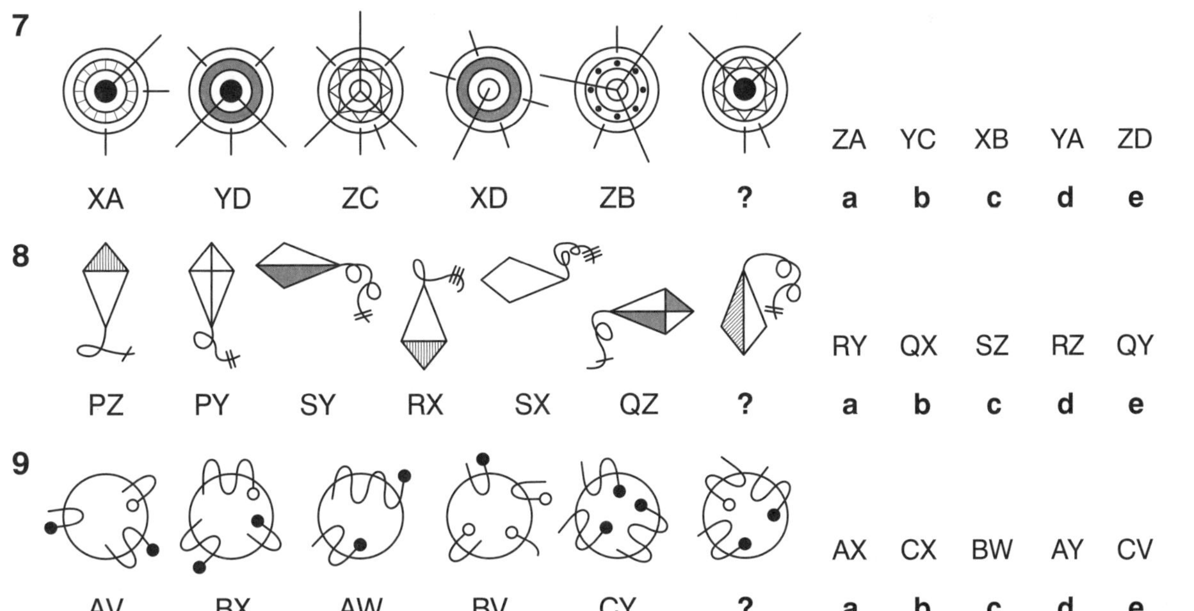

Which shape or pattern is made when the first two shapes or patterns are put together?

Example

\+ =

a b (c) d e

10 + =

a b c d e

11 + =

a b c d e

12 + =

a b c d e

Total

Test 14: **Mixed**

Test time: 0 5 10 minutes

Which pattern on the right belongs in the group on the left?

1

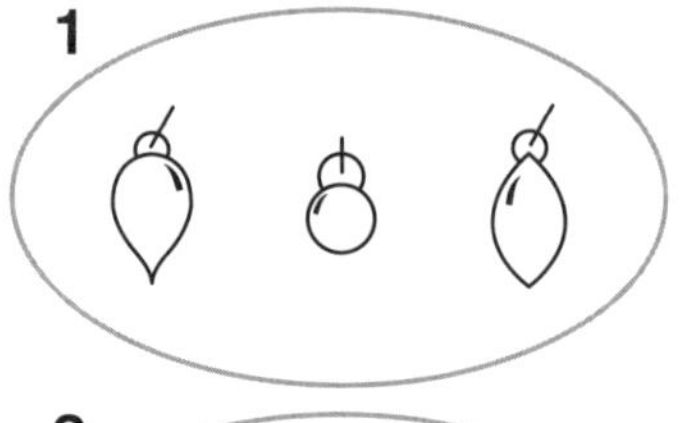

a

b

c

d

e

2

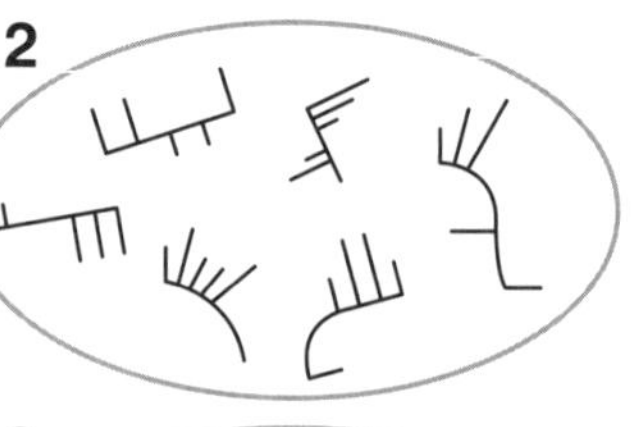

a b c d e

3

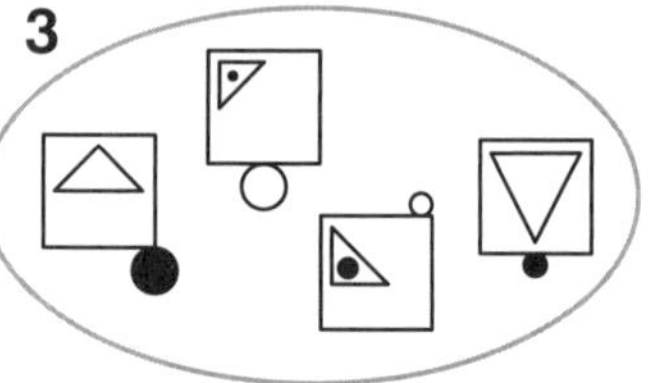

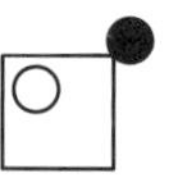
a

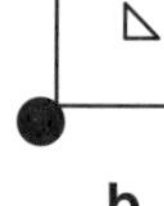
b

c

d

e

Which shape or pattern completes the larger square?

4

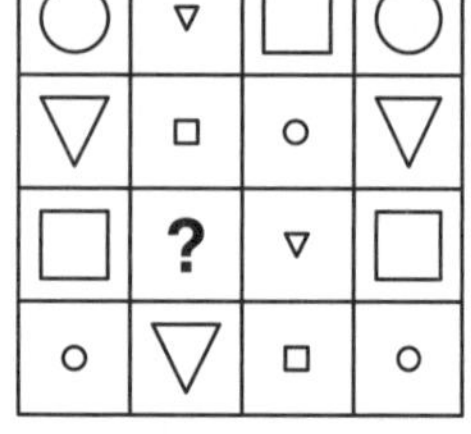

a

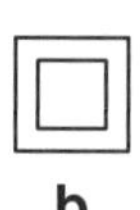
b

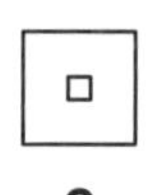
c

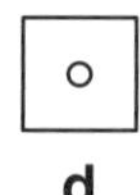
d

e

5

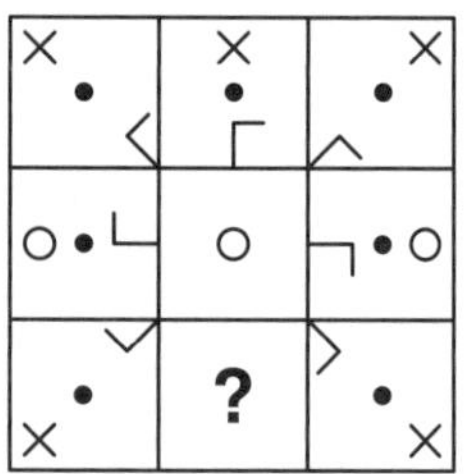

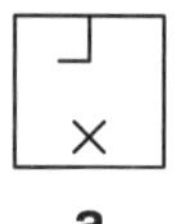
a

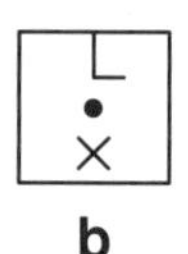
b

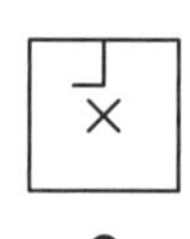
c

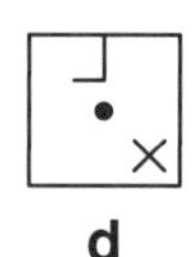
d

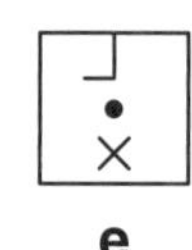
e

6

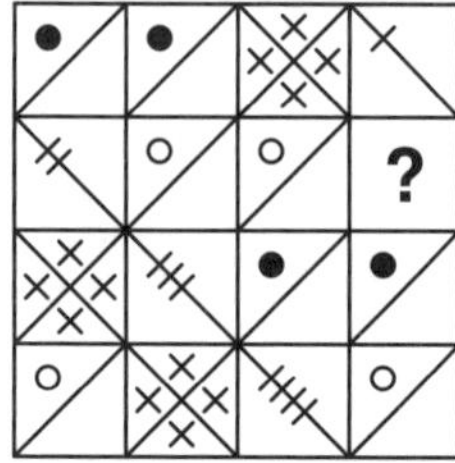

a

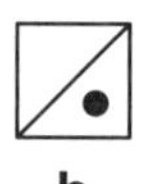
b

c

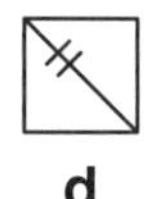
d

e

Which cube cannot be made from the given net?

7

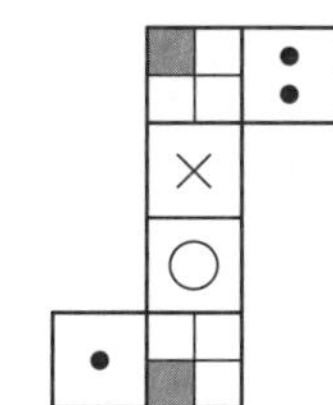

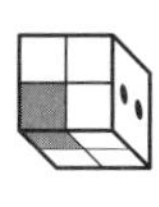

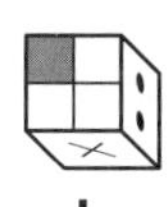

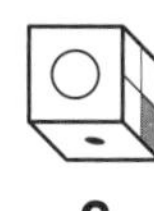

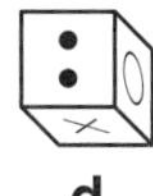

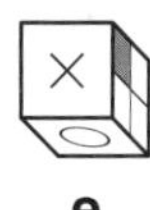

a b c d e

8

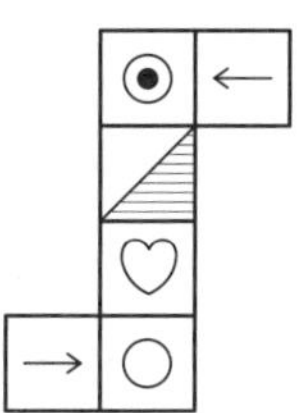

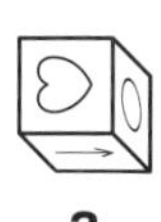

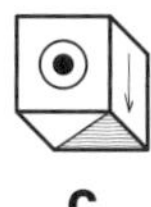

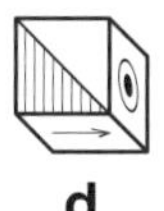

a b c d e

9

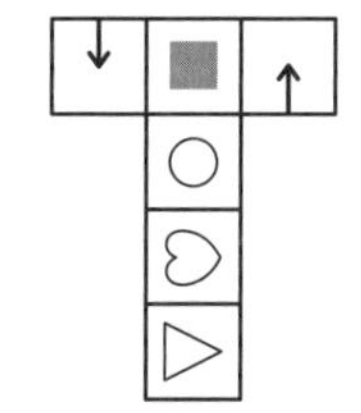

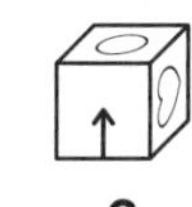

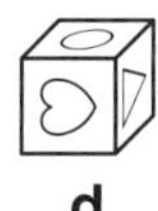

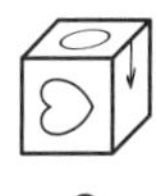

a b c d e

Which shape or pattern is made when the first two shapes or patterns are put together?

10

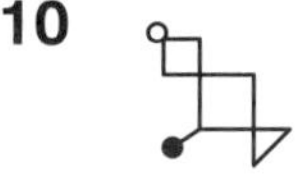

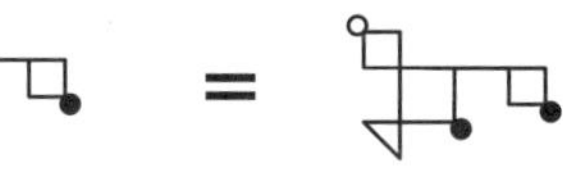

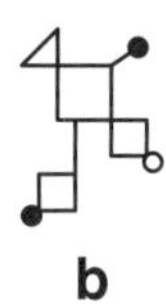

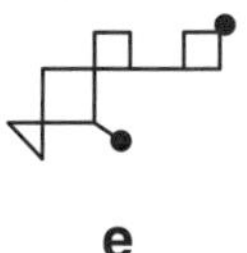

a b c d e

11

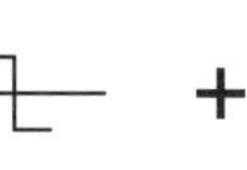

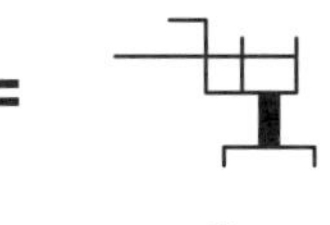

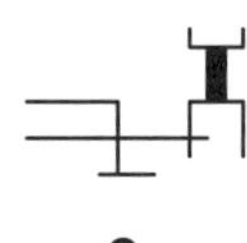

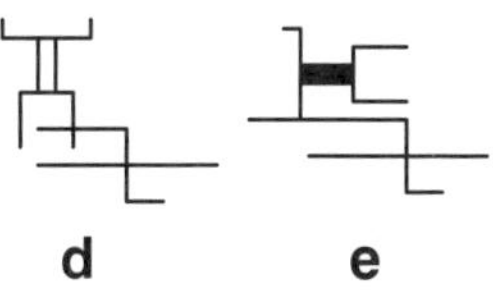

a b c d e

12

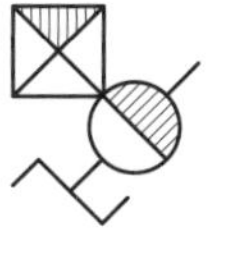

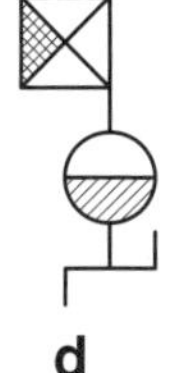

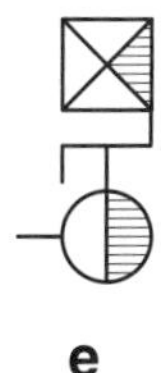

a b c d e

Total

TEST 15: **Mixed**

Which shape or pattern on the right completes the second pair in the same way as the first pair?

1 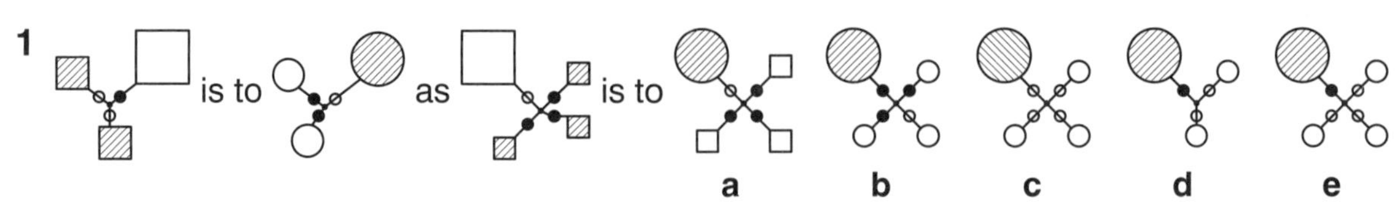

2 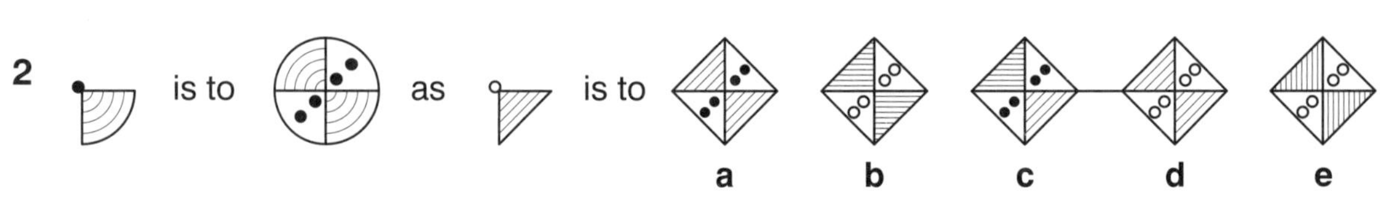

3 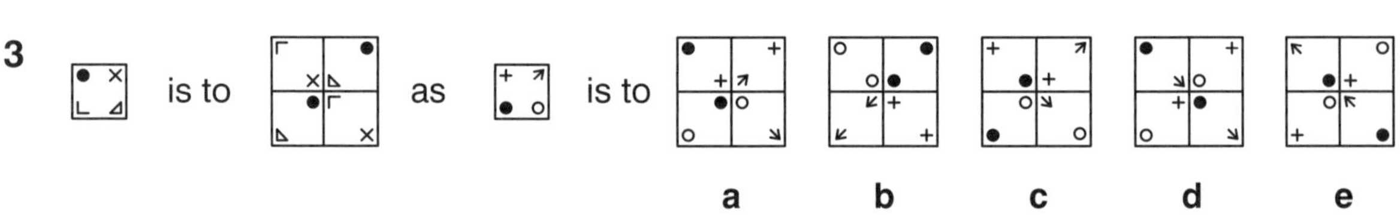

Which one comes next?

4 

5 

6 ?

a b c d e

Which cube cannot be made from the given net?

7

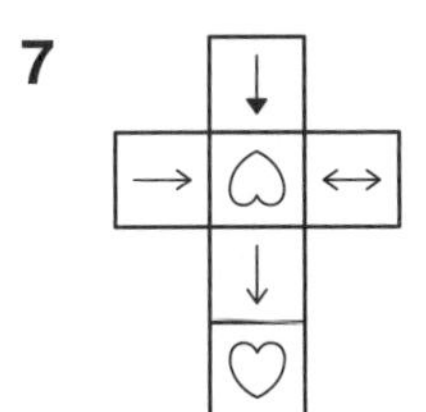

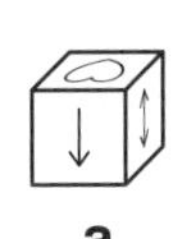
a

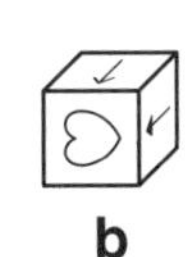
b

c

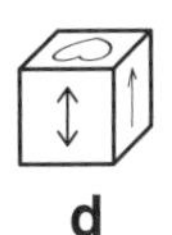
d

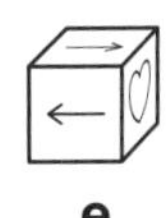
e

8

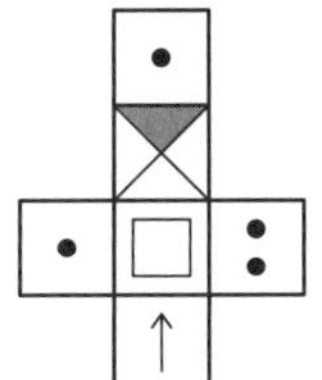

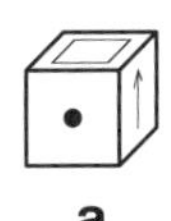
a

b

c

d

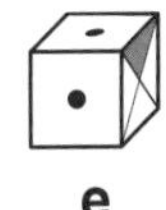
e

9

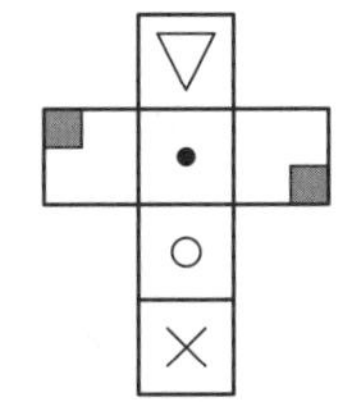

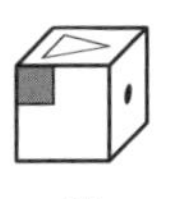
a

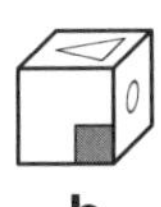
b

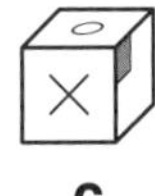
c

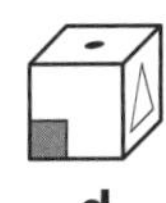
d

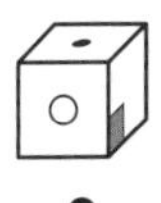
e

Which code matches the shape or pattern given at the end of each line?

10

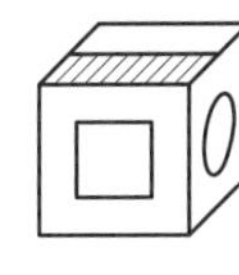
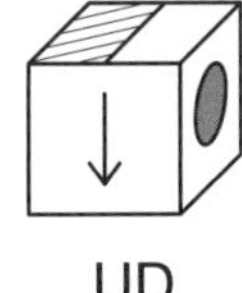

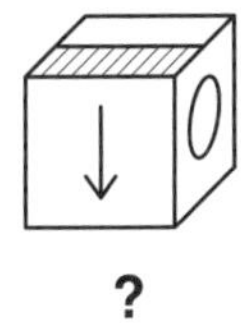

RB SC TA UD SB ?

TD	SA	RD	UA	TC
a	**b**	**c**	**d**	**e**

11

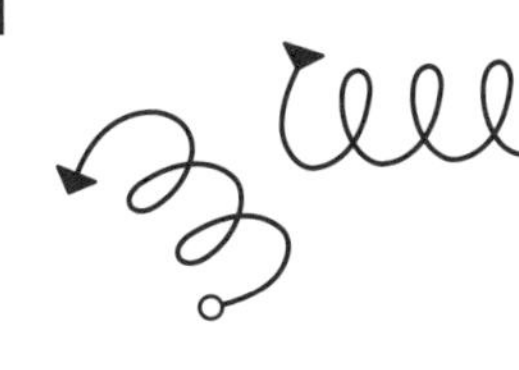
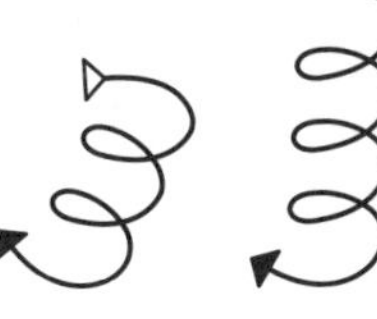

AR BP CQ DR CS ?

AS	BS	DP	BR	AQ
a	**b**	**c**	**d**	**e**

12

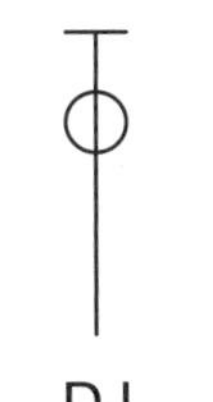

DJ FL GK EJ FK GM ?

EM	GL	EL	FJ	DK
a	**b**	**c**	**d**	**e**

Total

Test 16: **Mixed**

Test time: 0 5 10 minutes

Which pattern on the right belongs in the group on the left?

1

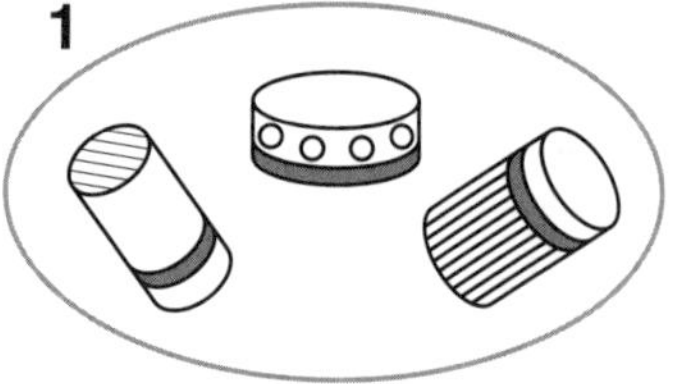

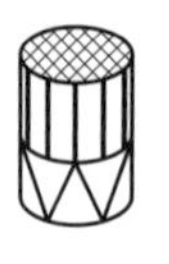
a

b

c

d

e

2

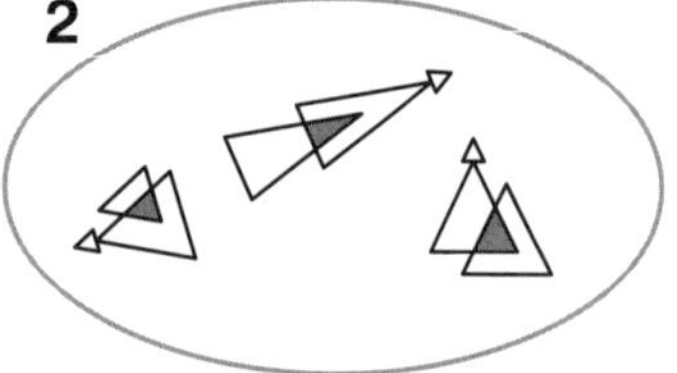

a

b

c

d

e

3

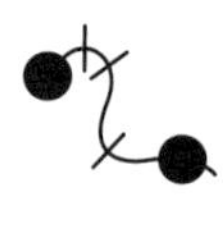
a

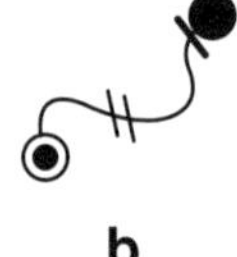
b

c

d

e

Which shape or pattern completes the larger square?

4

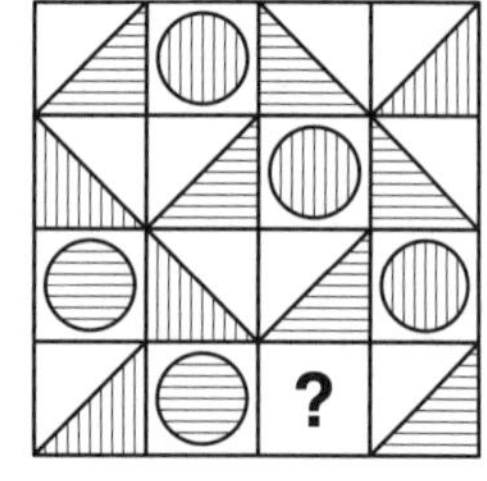

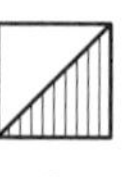
a

b

c

d

e

5

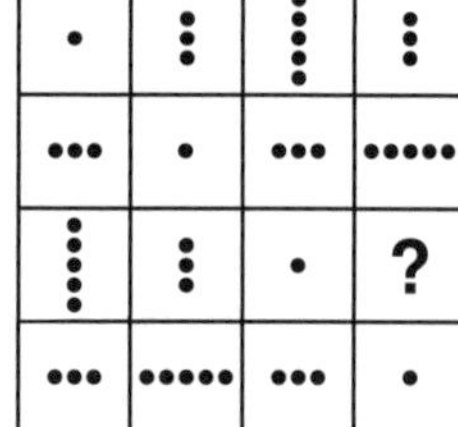

a

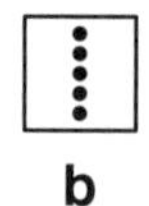
b

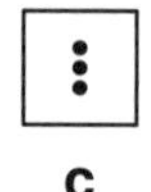
c

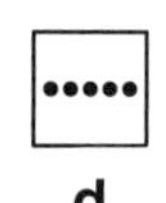
d

e

6

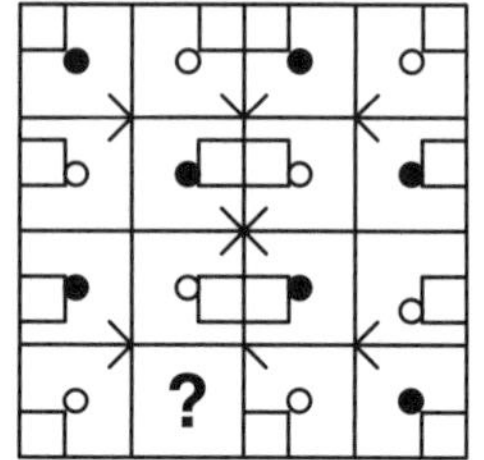

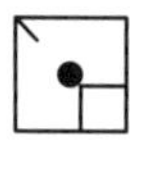
a

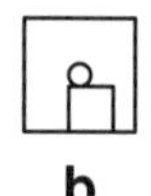
b

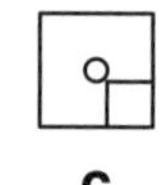
c

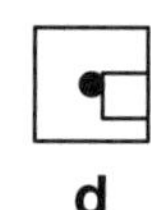
d

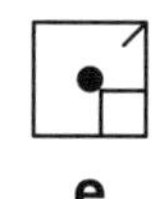
e

Which cube cannot be made from the given net?

7 

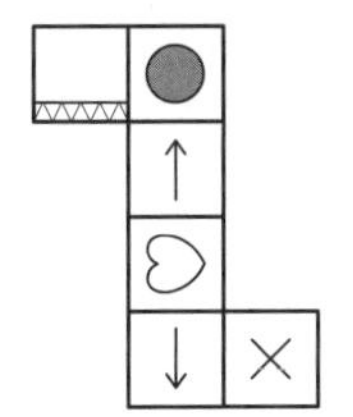

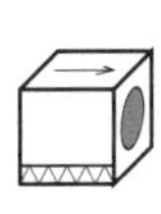
a

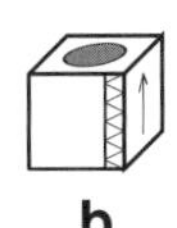
b

c

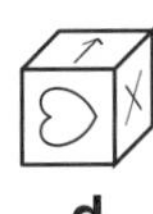
d

e

8

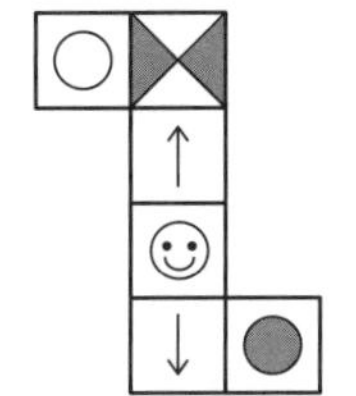

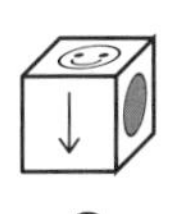
a

b

c

d

e

9

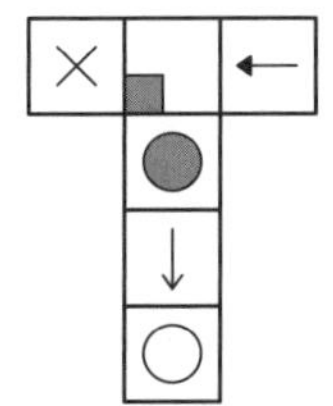

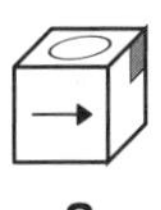
a

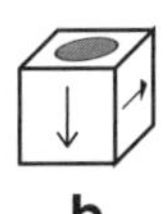
b

c

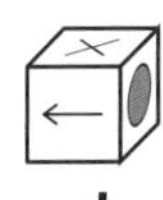
d

e

Which shape or pattern is made when the first two shapes or patterns are put together?

10

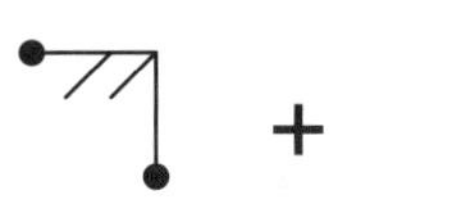

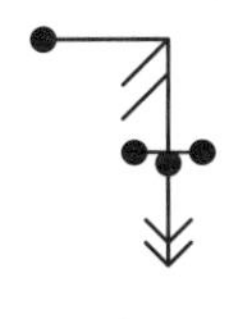
a

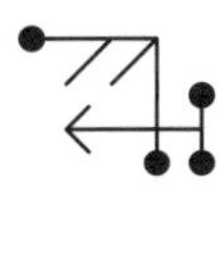
b

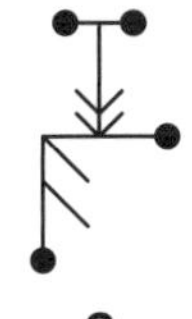
c

d

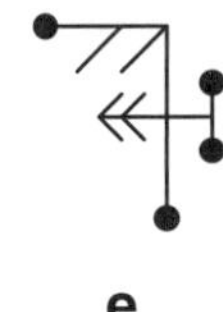
e

11

a

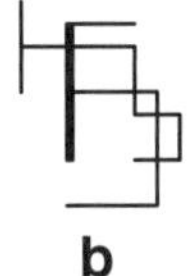
b

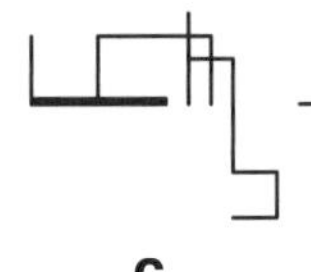
c

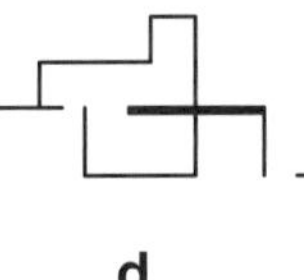
d

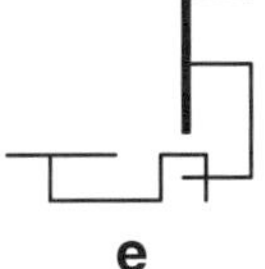
e

12

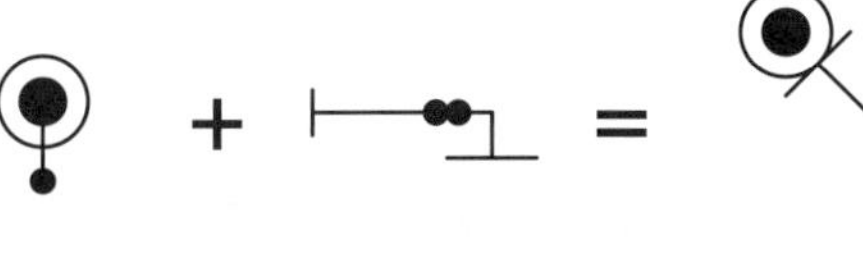

a

b

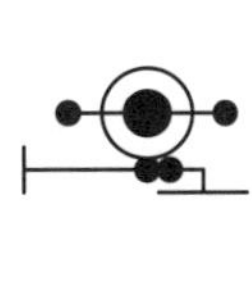
c

d

e

Time for a break! Go to Puzzle Page 45

Total

Test 17: **Mixed**

Test time: 0 5 10 minutes

Which pattern on the right belongs in the group on the left?

1

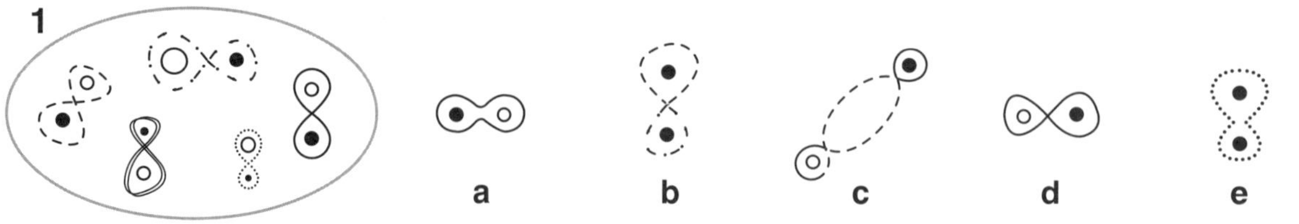

a
b
c
d
e

2

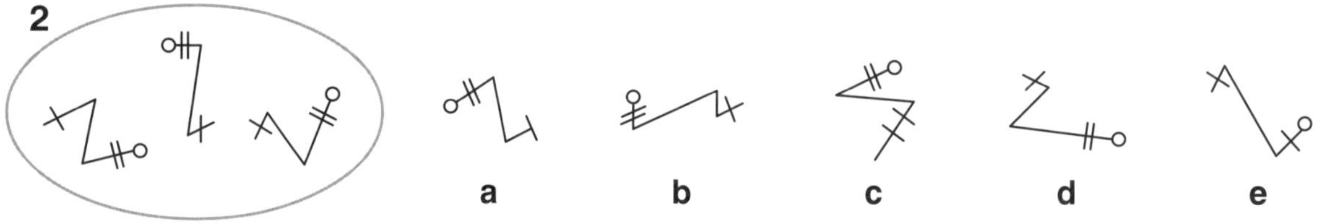

a
b
c
d
e

3

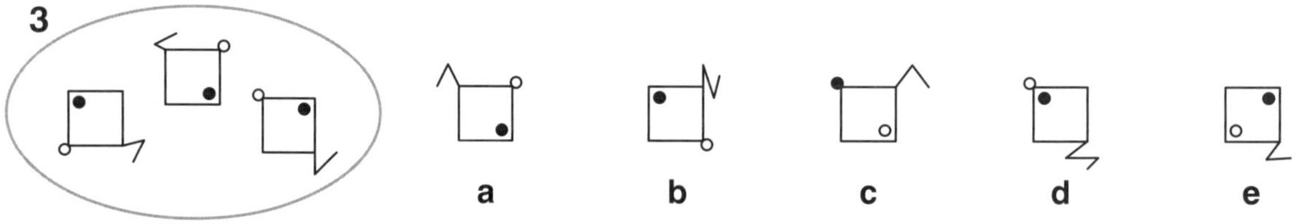

a
b
c
d
e

Which shape or pattern on the right completes the second pair in the same way as the first pair?

4

is to
as
is to
a
b
c
d
e

5

is to
as
is to
a
b
c
d
e

6

is to
as
is to
a
b
c
d
e

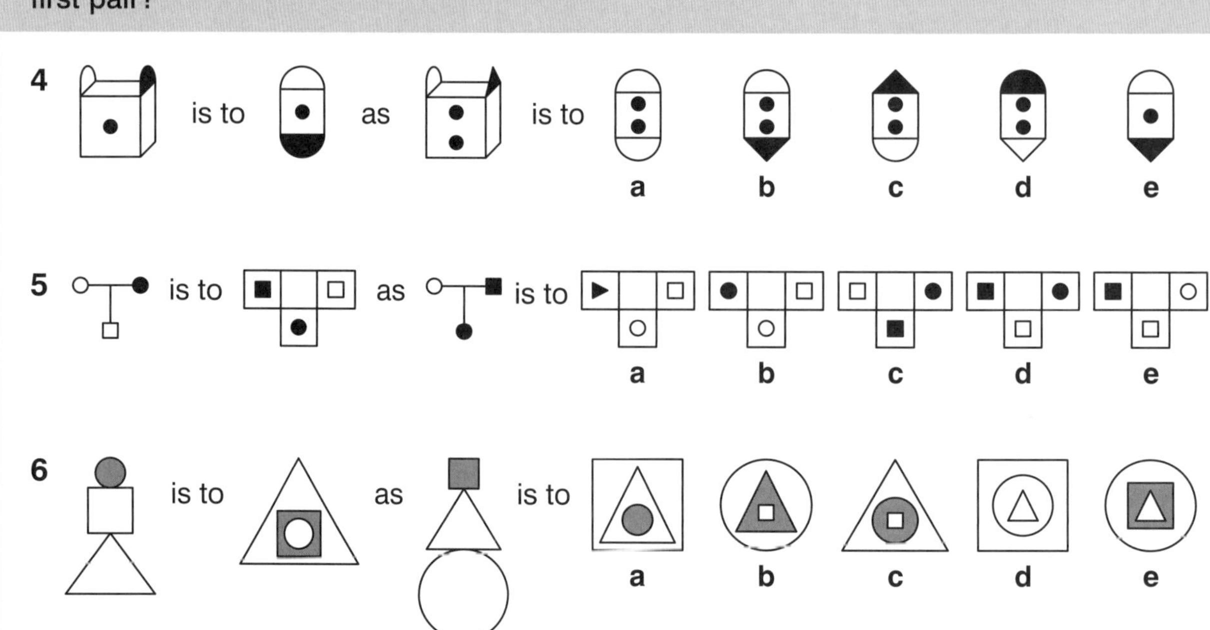

Which one comes next?

7

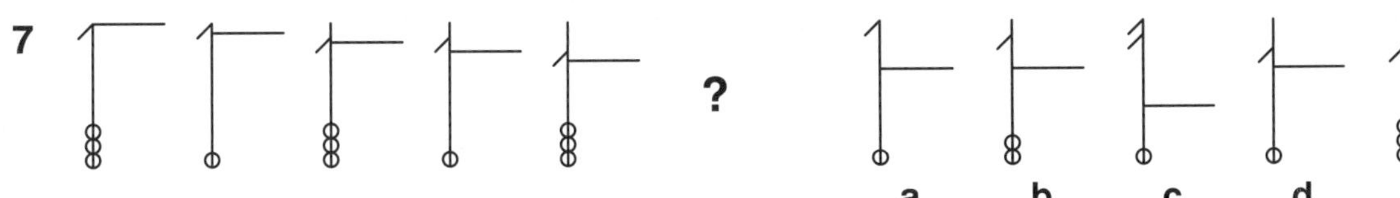

?

a b c d e

8

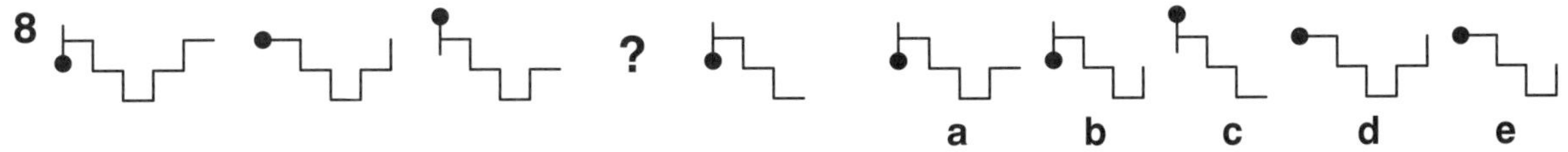

?

a b c d e

9

?

a b c d e

Which code matches the shape or pattern given at the end of each line?

10

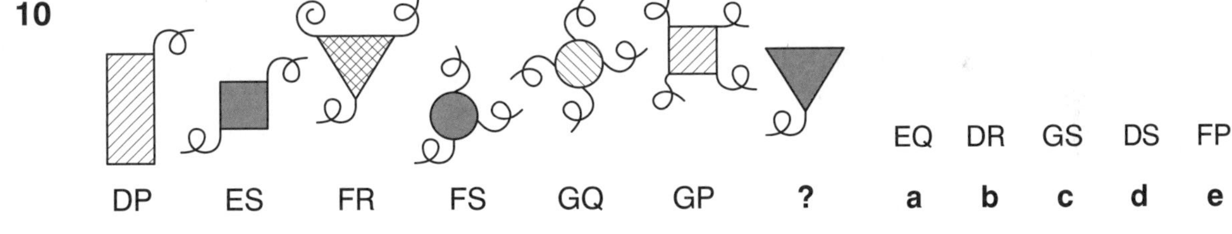

DP ES FR FS GQ GP ?

EQ DR GS DS FP

a b c d e

11

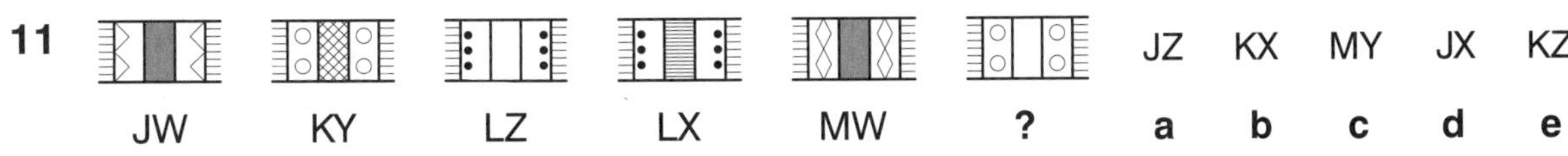

JW KY LZ LX MW ?

JZ KX MY JX KZ

a b c d e

12

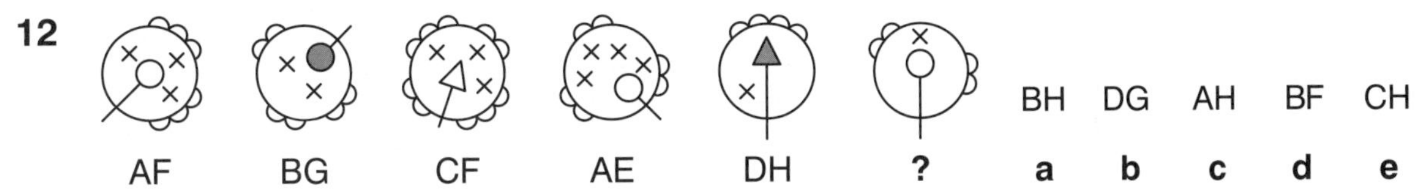

AF BG CF AE DH ?

BH DG AH BF CH

a b c d e

Total

Test 18: **Mixed**

Test time: 0 5 10 minutes

Which pattern on the right belongs in the group on the left?

1

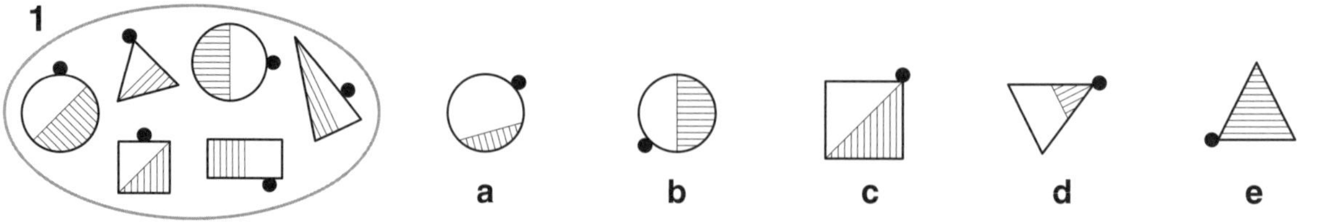

a b c d e

2

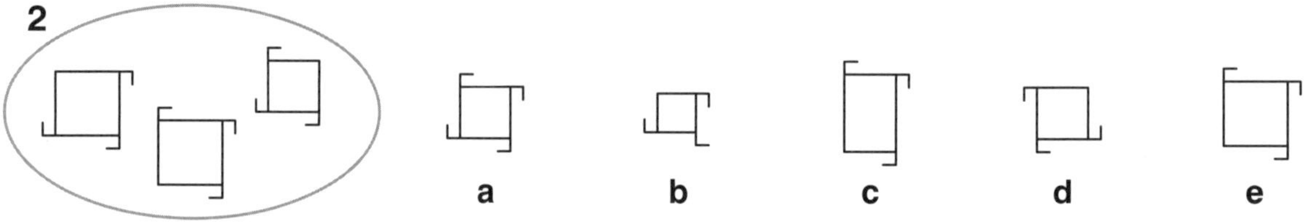

a b c d e

3

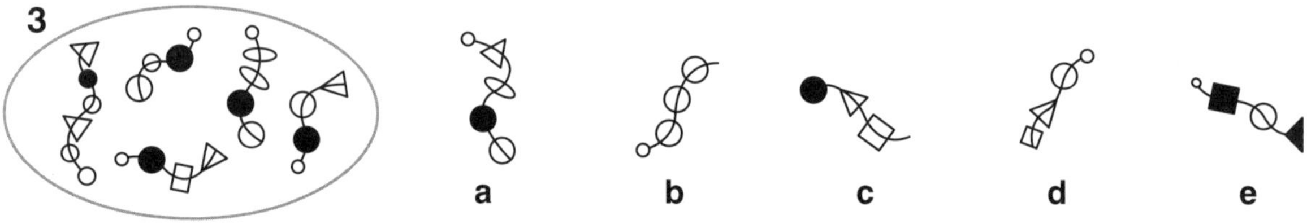

a b c d e

Which shape on the right is the reflection of the shape given on the left?

4

a b c d e

5

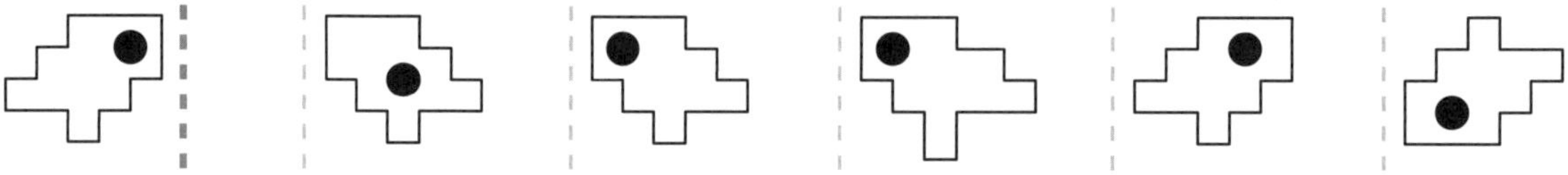

a b c d e

6

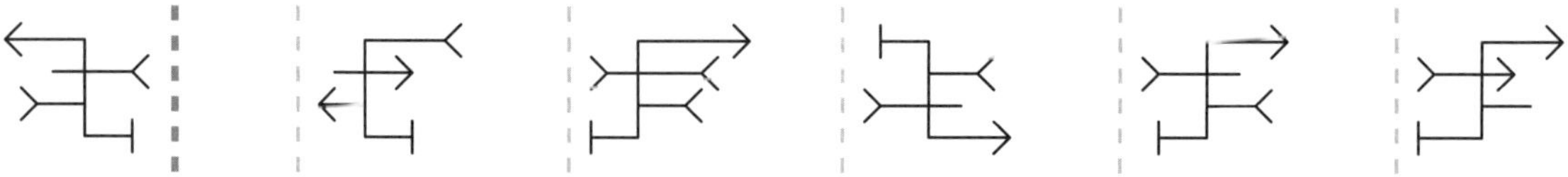

a b c d e

Which cube cannot be made from the given net?

7

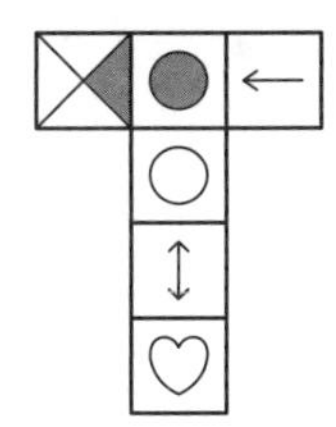   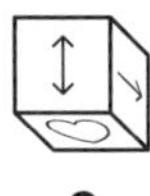 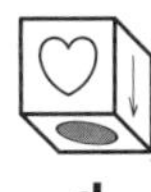  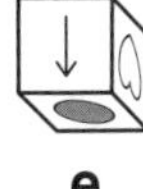

a **b** **c** **d** **e**

8

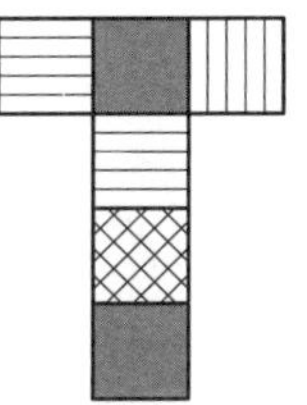 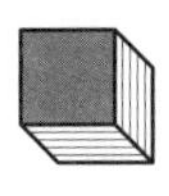 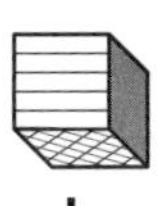  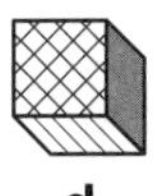 

a **b** **c** **d** **e**

9

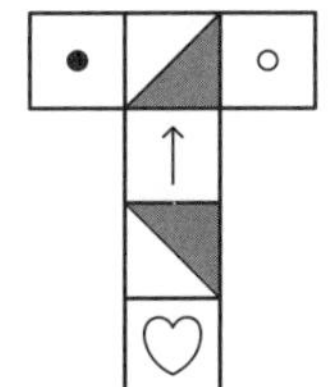 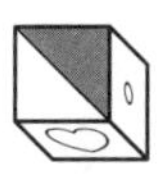 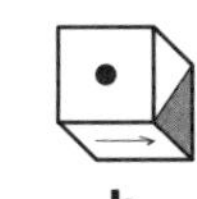 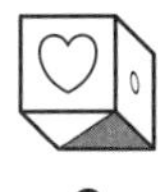 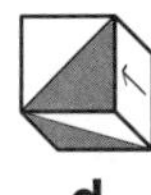 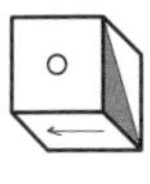

a **b** **c** **d** **e**

Which shape or pattern is made when the first two shapes or patterns are put together?

10

 + 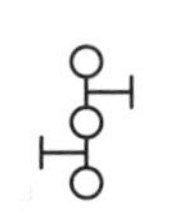 = 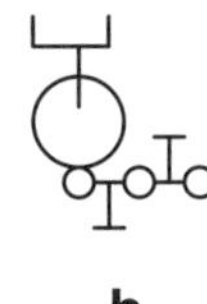 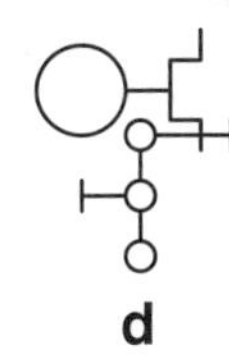 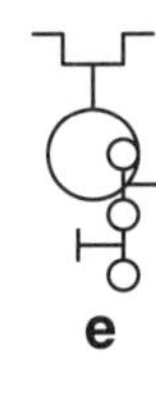

a **b** **c** **d** **e**

11

 +  = 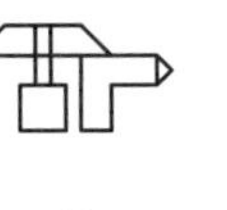 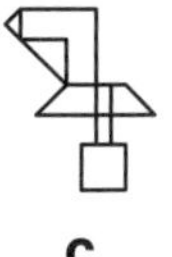 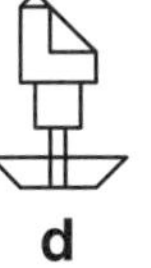 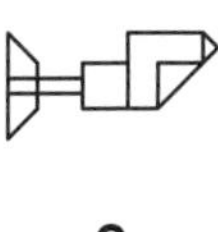

a **b** **c** **d** **e**

12

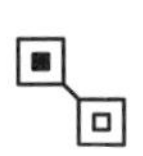 +  = 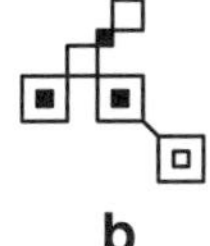  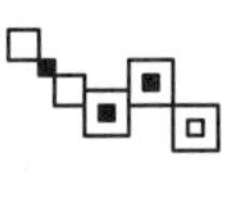 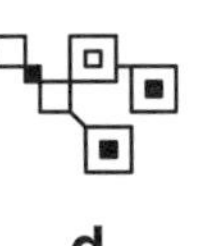 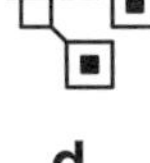 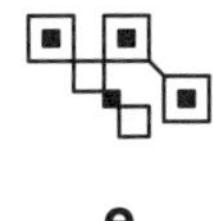

a **b** **c** **d** **e**

Total

TEST 19: **Mixed**

Test time: 0 5 10 minutes

Which shape or pattern on the right completes the second pair in the same way as the first pair?

1 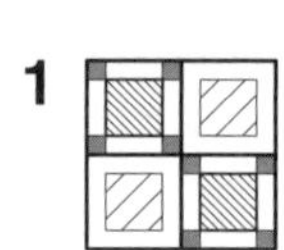 is to 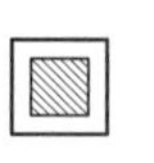 as 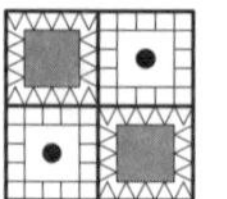 is to

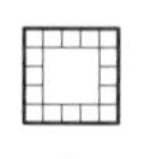 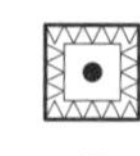 

a b c d e

2 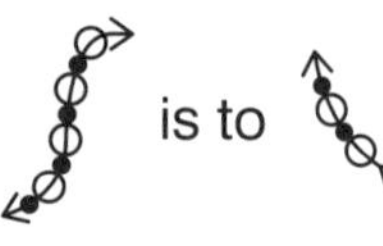 is to as is to

a b c d e

3 is to  as  is to

a b c d e

Which one comes next?

4   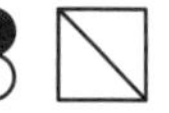  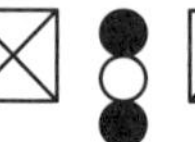 ?

a b c d e

5  ?

a b c d e

6  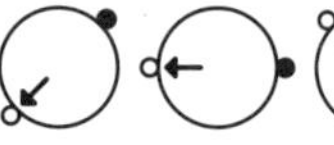  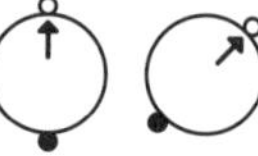 ?

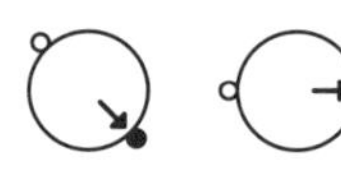   

a b c d e

Which cube cannot be made from the given net?

7

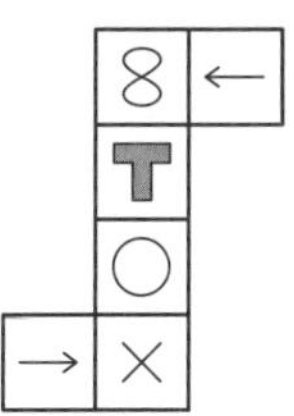

 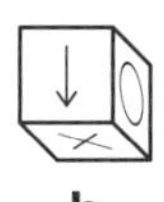  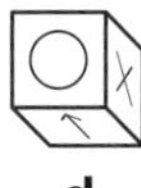 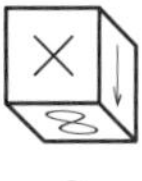

a **b** **c** **d** **e**

8

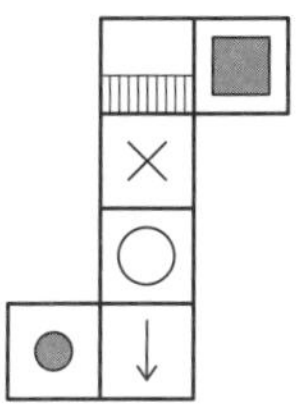

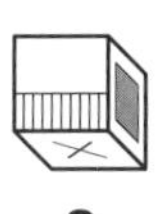 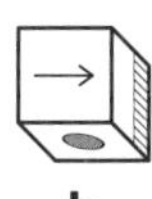  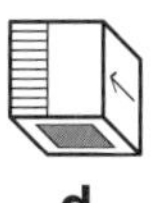 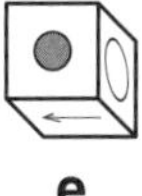

a **b** **c** **d** **e**

9

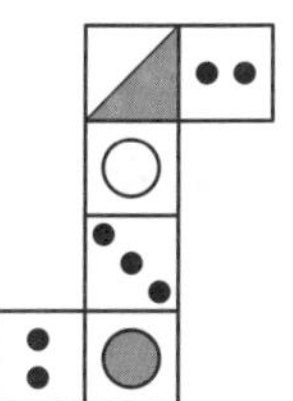

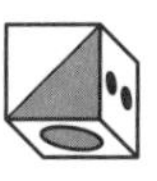  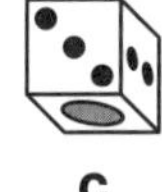 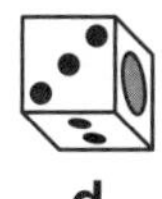 

a **b** **c** **d** **e**

Which code matches the shape or pattern given at the end of each line?

10

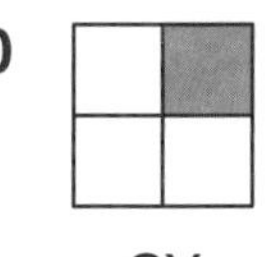 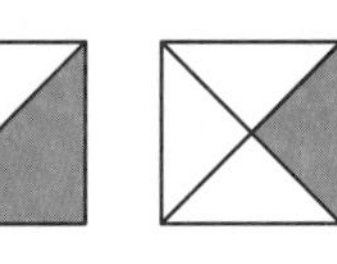 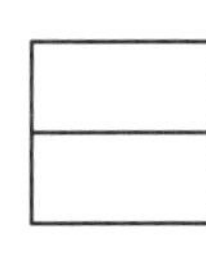 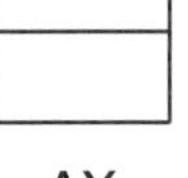 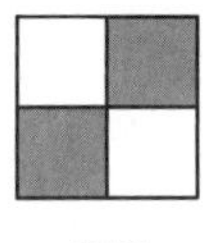  

CY BZ DY AX CZ ?

AZ CX BY DZ DX

a **b** **c** **d** **e**

11

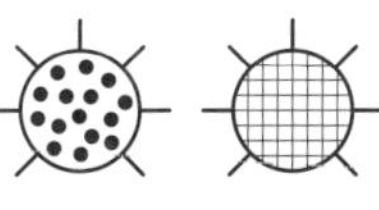  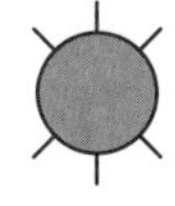 

DM DN EM FO EO GL ?

GM DL GN FN DO

a **b** **c** **d** **e**

12

 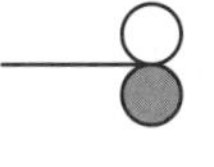 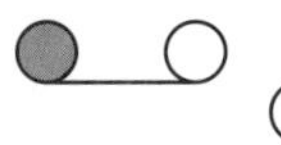 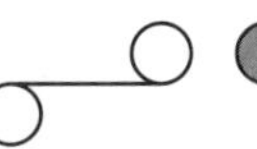 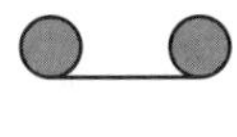

RE TG UF SF TE ?

RG SG UE SE TF

a **b** **c** **d** **e**

Total

Test 20: **Mixed**

Test time: 0 5 10 minut

Which pattern on the right belongs in the group on the left?

1

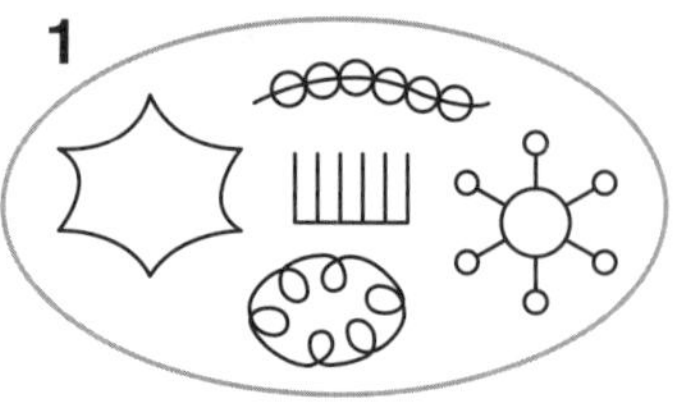

a

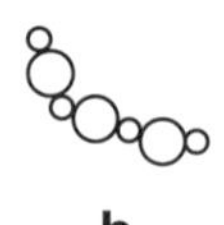

b

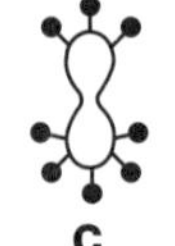

c

d

e

2

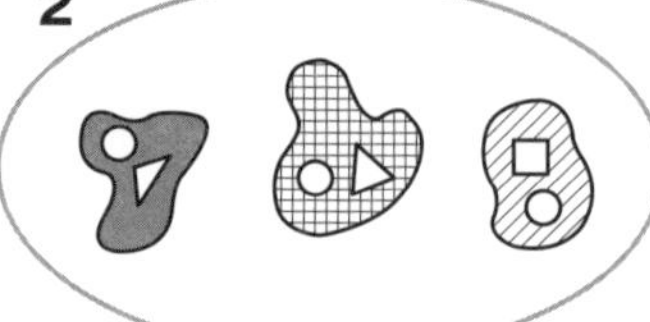

a

b

c

d

e

3

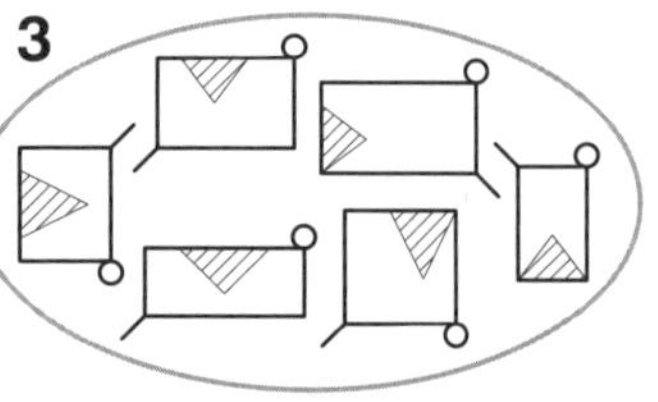

a

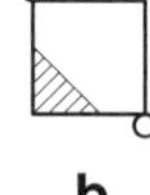

b

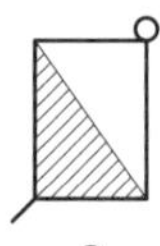

c

d

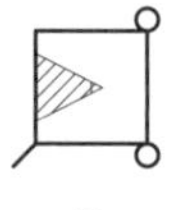

e

Which shape or pattern on the right completes the second pair in the same way as the first pair?

4 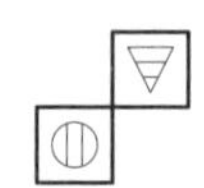 is to  as 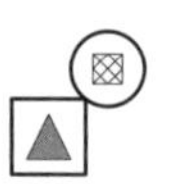 is to

a

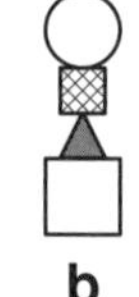

b

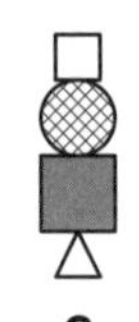

c

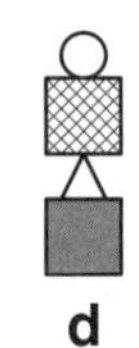

d

e

5  is to as  is to

a

b

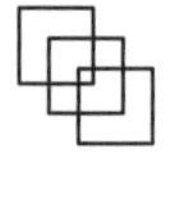

c

d e

6  is to  as  is to

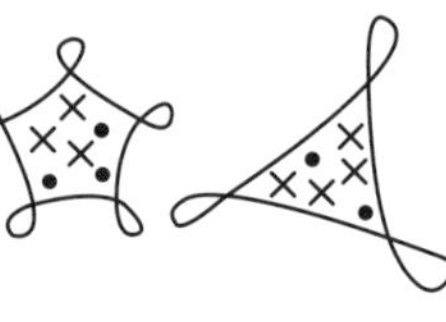

a b c

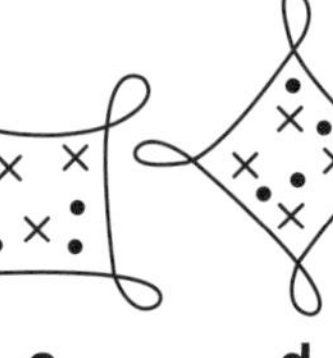

d e

Which shape on the right is the reflection of the shape given on the left?

7

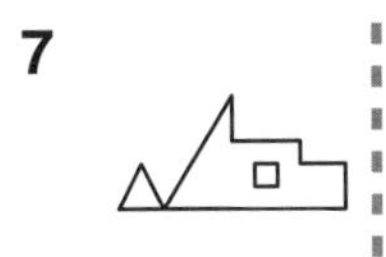

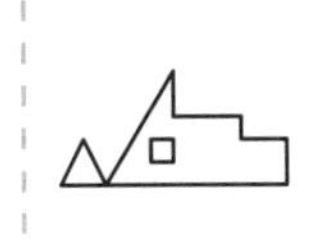
a

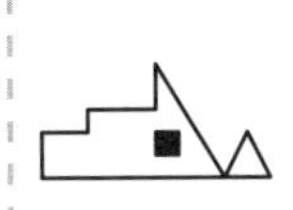
b

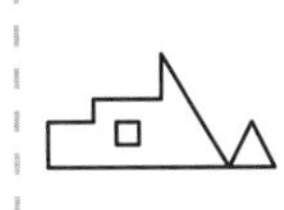
c

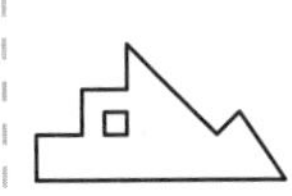
d

e

8

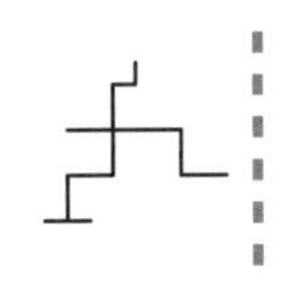

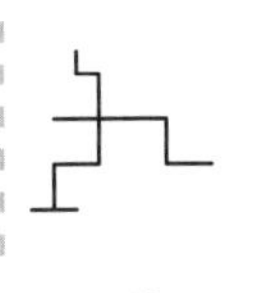
a

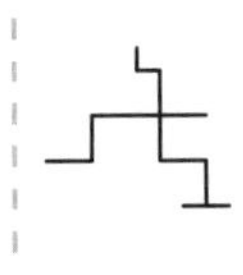
b

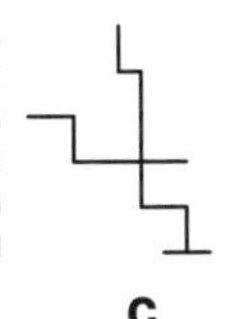
c

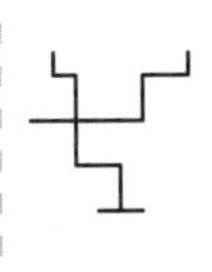
d

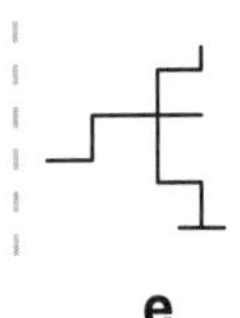
e

9

a

b

c

d

e

Which cube cannot be made from the given net?

10

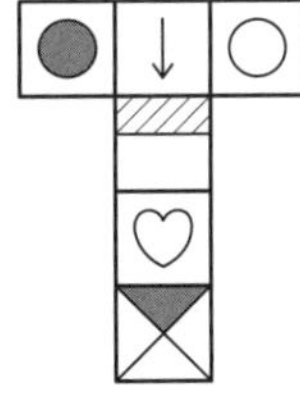

a

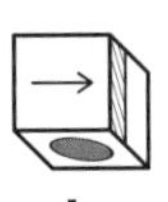
b

c

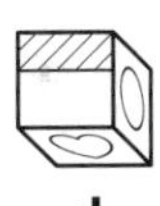
d

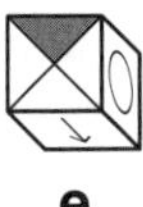
e

11

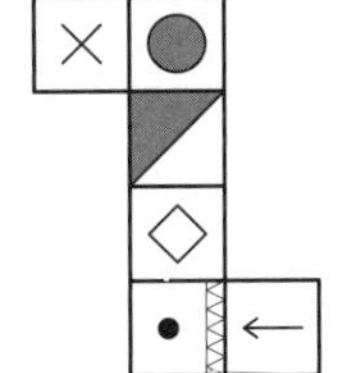

a

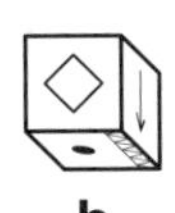
b

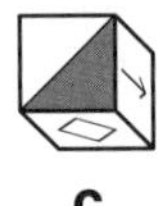
c

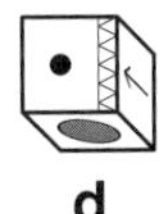
d

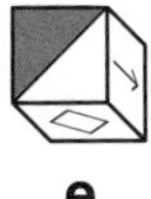
e

12

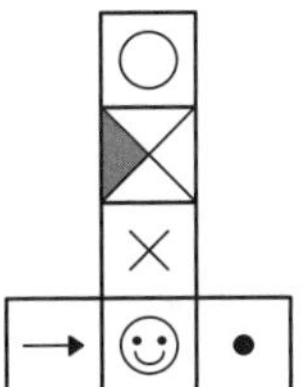

a

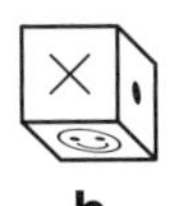
b

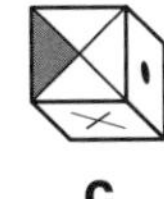
c

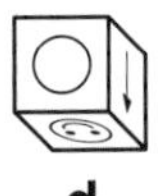
d

e

Time for a break! Go to Puzzle Page 46

Total

Puzzle 1

Decide which numbered piece fits in the missing squares on the puzzles.

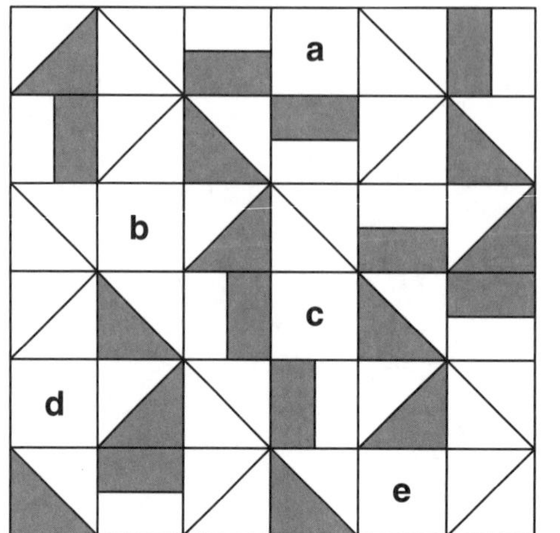

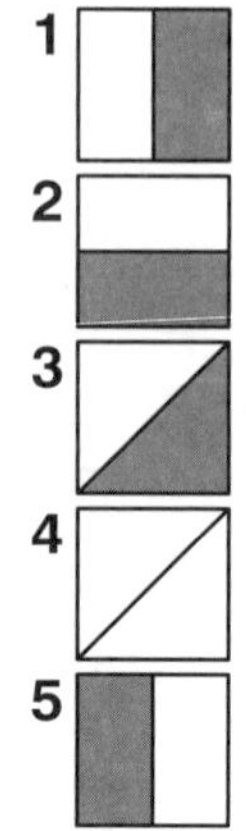

a =

b =

c =

d =

e =

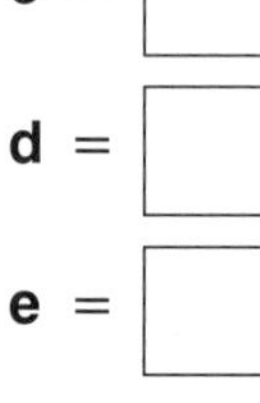

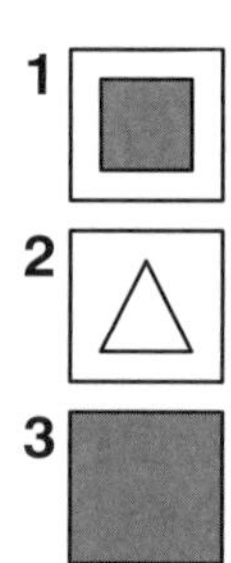

a =

b =

c =

d =

e =

f =

g =

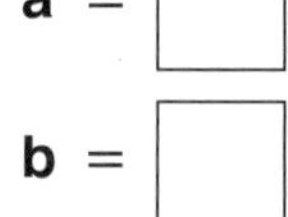

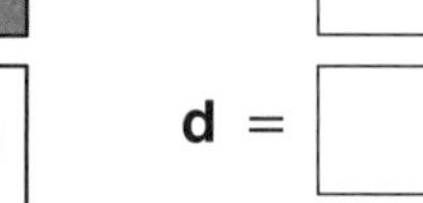

Puzzle 2

In the set of shapes below, there are six different types of shapes. Each type of shape appears three times. Identify the identical shapes – you may want to draw a circle around one set of identical shapes, a square around another set, etc.

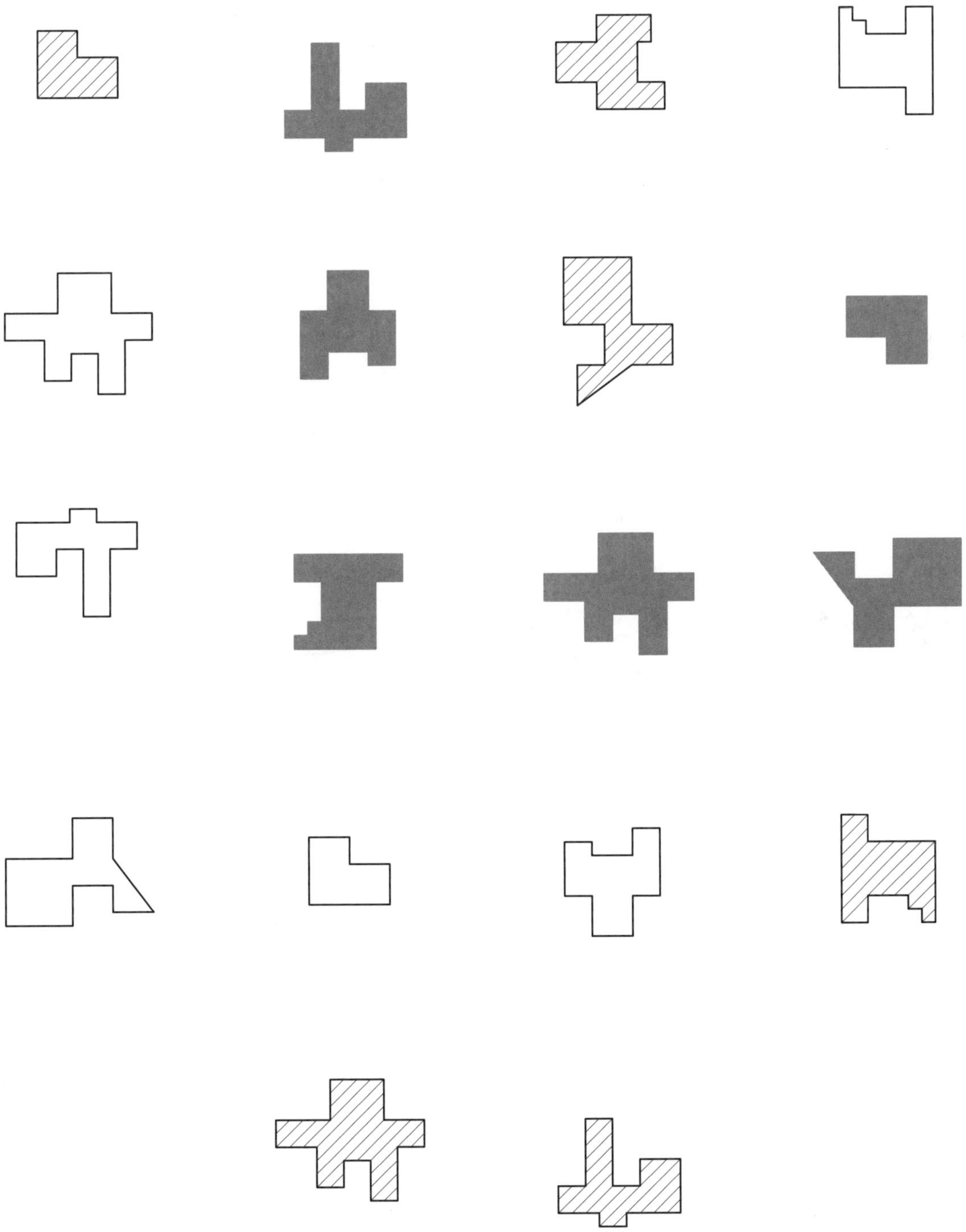

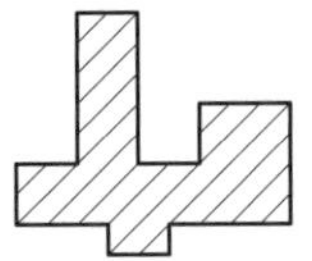

Puzzle ❸

Continue the pattern on these rows of beads.

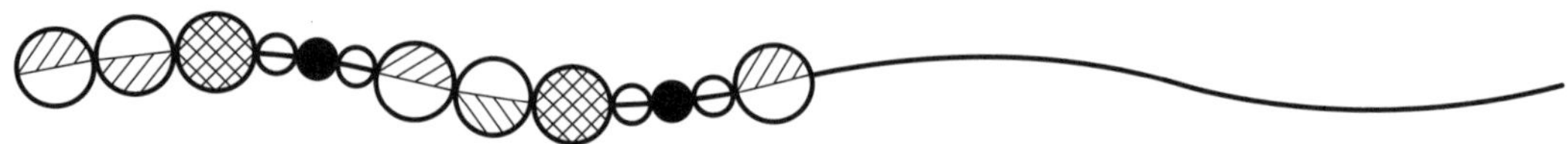

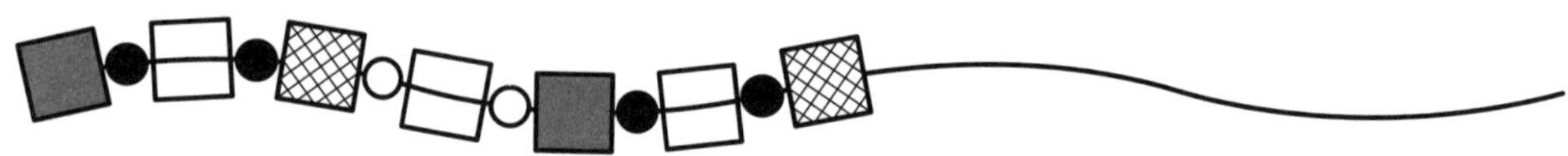

Puzzle 4

Complete these patterns by drawing their reflection in the dotted mirror lines.

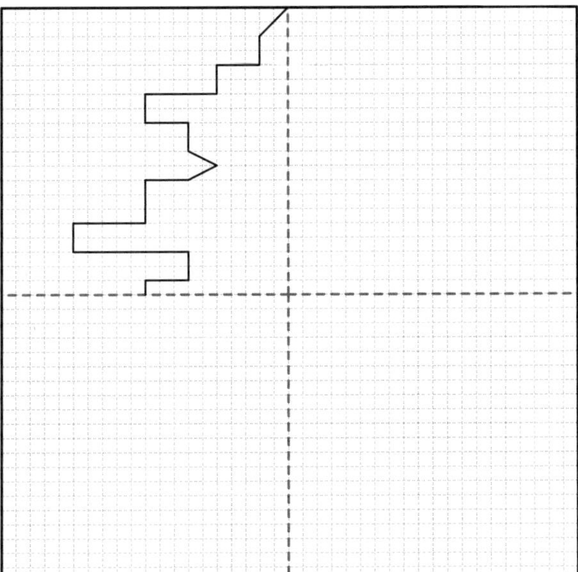

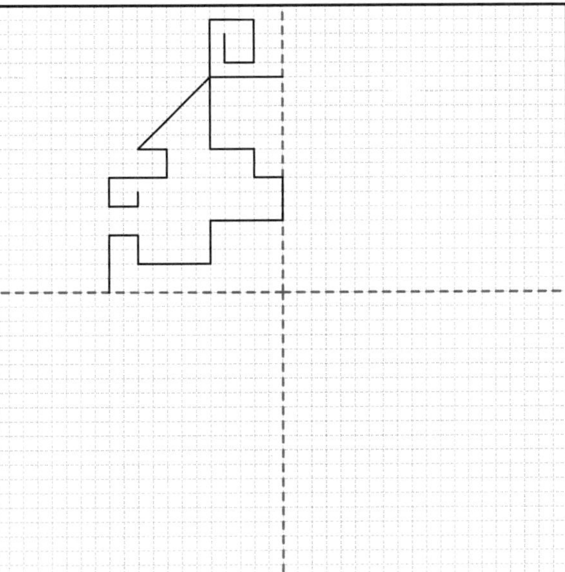

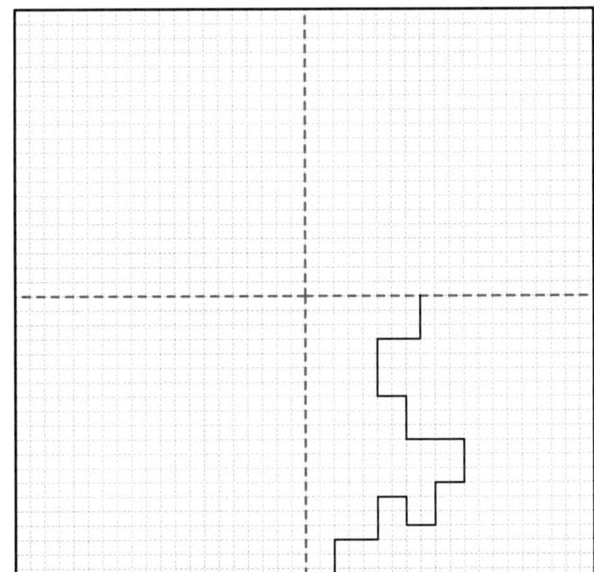

Puzzle 5

Here are some messages written in code. Use the codes to work out what the messages say. An alphabet line is provided to help.

A B C D E F G H I J K L M N O P Q R S T U V W X Y Z

Code 1 CAT = ECV

What does this message say?

OGGV OG CV VJG RCTM VQFCA

Code 2 WEST = VDRS

OKDZRD BNLD SN LX OZQSX SNLNQQNV

Code 3 SEAT = PBXQ

QEBOB FP DLIA XQ QEB YLQQLJ LC LRO DXOABK!

Code 1: ....

Code 2: ....

....

Code 3: ....

....

Now try writing your own messages in code and get a friend to decode them.

Progress Grid Non-verbal Reasoning 10 Minute Tests 11^+–12^+ years

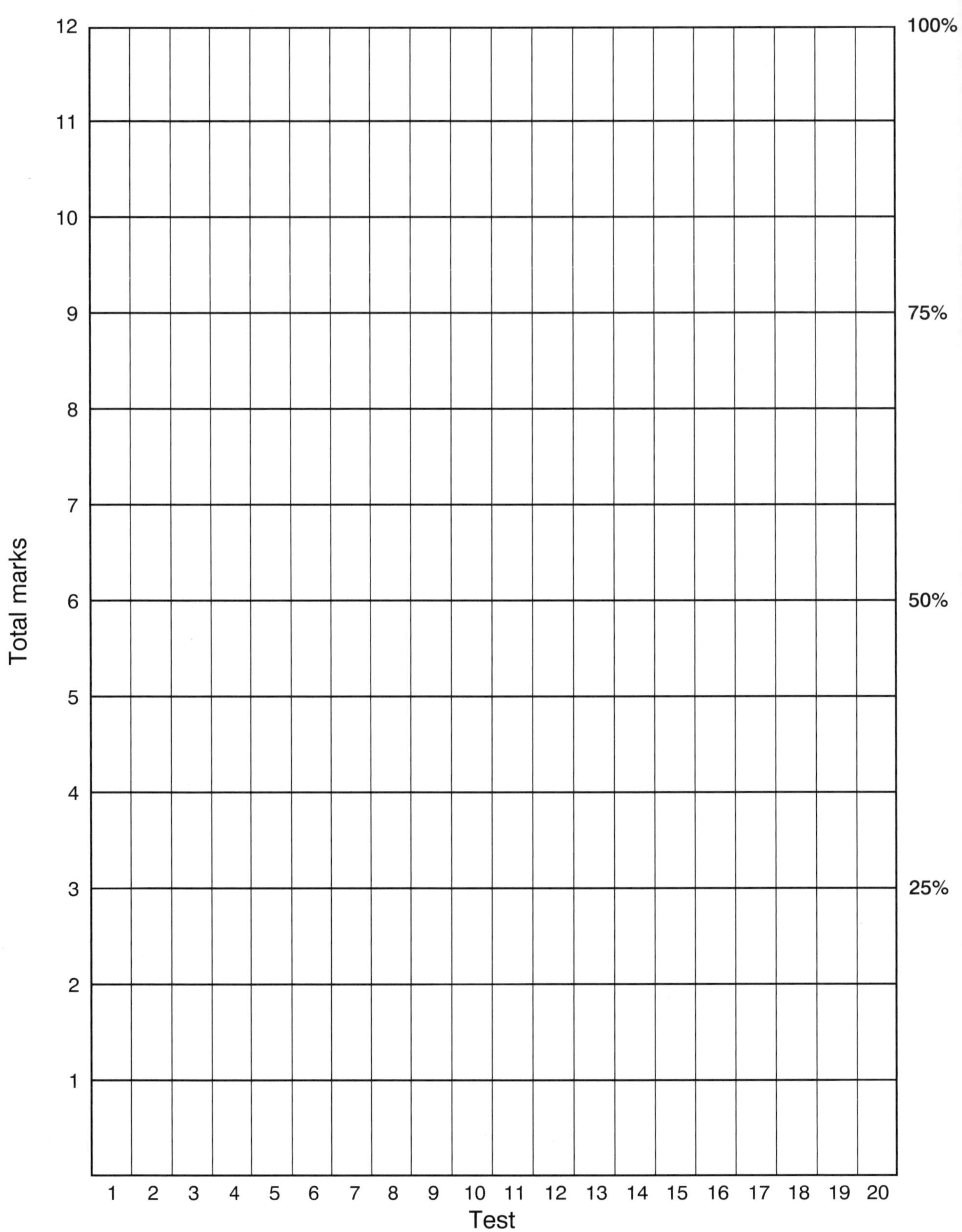